Mike
our hunting
escapades would
make another good
book — Enjoy
Steve

DAWN OF AMERICAN
DEER HUNTING

A PHOTOGRAPHIC ODYSSEY OF WHITETAIL HUNTING HISTORY

DUNCAN DOBIE

Published by

Krause Publications a division of F+W Media, Inc.
700 East State Street • Iola, WI 54990-0001
715-445-2214 • 888-457-2873
www.krausebooks.com

To order books or other products call toll-free 1-800-258-0929
or visit us online at www.shopdeerhunting.com

All photos and graphics, unless noted, are credited to
Duncan Dobie's personal collection.

ISBN-13: 978-1-4402-4551-0
ISBN-10: 1-4402-4551-7

Designed by Dane Royer
Edited by Chris Berens

Printed in China

10 9 8 7 6 5 4 3 2 1

For Kappi, who has put up with my obsession
for old black and white photos for way too long.

ABOUT THE AUTHOR

Duncan Dobie has been a full-time outdoor writer for more than 30 years. His stories and photographs have appeared in numerous books, magazines and newspapers across the country, most of which cover whitetails and whitetail hunting. He has authored nine books, and seven are about white-tailed deer. Among his most recent books are *Hunting Mature Whitetails the Lakosky Way*, *Legendary Whitetails III* and *Trophy Whitetails with Pat and Nicole Reeve*, all three with Krause Publications. Duncan lives in Marietta, Georgia.

CONTENTS

TWO AMERICAN ORIGINALS

The happy grin on his face says it all. With his trusty Savage, that could no doubt tell a few tales of its own, and a fine set of trophy antlers that will soon occupy a prominent place in his room for years to come, young Noel Thompson of Washington state couldn't be prouder.

According to records, Noel was born in Centralia, Salzer Creek, Wash., (just south of Olympia) in 1890. He died in 1970 at age 80. The photo was probably taken between 1905 and 1910 when young Noel would have been between 16 and 20 years old. His worn boots and the weathered barn behind him indicate that Noel was a hardy farm boy. Hopefully he enjoyed a long life of whitetail hunting.

Interestingly, the skull and antlers Noel is holding are probably those of a somewhat rare Columbian whitetail, the westernmost subspecies of whitetails found in North America that range in a relatively small area along the Pacific coast of Washington and Oregon. Noted by Lewis and Clark in 1806 and originally called the "common red deer" by the expedition members, as opposed to the "black-tailed fallow deer" (blacktails) they also encountered, the expedition later referred to the common red deer as "that little deer with the white tail."

Never very numerous to start with, the population of Columbian whitetails dropped significantly to several hundred animals during the early part of the 20th century due to overhunting and poaching. Noel lived to see these deer placed on the endangered species list in 1968, joining the diminutive Florida Key Deer as the only two subspecies of whitetails ever to be federally protected under the Endangered Species Act. Thanks to good protection and management, Columbian whitetails were delisted in July 2003 in Douglas County in southwest Oregon. While these deer are still protected in some parts of Oregon and Washington, limited hunting has once again opened for these American originals in the Douglas County area.

TELLING THE WHITETAIL STORY THROUGH PHOTOGRAPHS

There is no question that whitetail hunting is a huge part of our American heritage. White-tailed deer were a gift to American pioneers and settlers. Today they are a gift to modern American hunters. Throughout our colonization and up to the mid-1800s, the only way to preserve this important part of our heritage was through various art forms, the written word and traditional storytelling. But shortly after photography was invented and continually improved upon during the middle and late 19th century, something amazing happened. People started recording whitetail hunting with photographs.

Shortly after the Civil War, thousands of photos were taken of whitetail hunters plying their trade in most places where deer existed. Many of those photos survive today and they give us considerable insight into how things were in the late 1800s and early 1900s. Stereoscopes, also known as stereopticons or stereoviewers, were one of America's most popular forms of entertainment in the late 1800s, and deer hunting was well represented in the parlors and living rooms of America through this medium.

The first patented stereoscope was invented by Sir Charles Wheatstone in 1838. A stereoscope is composed of two pictures mounted next to each other, and a set of lenses through which to view the pictures. Each picture is taken from a slightly different viewpoint that corresponds closely to the spacing of the eyes. The left picture represents what the left eye would see, and likewise for the right picture. When observing the pictures through a special viewer, the pair of two-dimensional pictures merge into a single photograph.

Wheatstone had experimented with simple stereoscopic drawings in 1832, several years before photography was invented. Later, the two principles were combined to form the stereoscope. Deer hunting stereoviews first started showing up in the 1870s. They remained popular from about 1880 to 1910. Shortly after the turn of the century, black and white photos and "cabinet photos" made from glass negatives began to replace stereoviews. Printed black and white postcards depicting deer hunting scenes also became very popular. Within a few years, these postcards were being colorized.

When we sportsmen walk into a Bass Pro Shop, Cabela's or Gander Mountain store, who doesn't stop and gawk at all of the old hunting and fishing photos on the walls? Like many hunters, I have always been fascinated with old deer hunting photos and our amazing American deer hunting heritage. When I see an old photo, I immediately start wondering about what life was like back in the day. A thousand questions pop into my head. How did hunters stay warm in the frigid cold, what kind of guns did they prefer and what kind of methods did they use 100 years ago? Often these snapshots from the past are self-explanatory. And as they answer certain questions, they begin to tell a special story. Years ago I started collecting old hunting photos because of my passion for the subject, and this book is the result of that almost lifelong interest.

If you happen to notice that the majority of the photos in this book are very regional, there is a good explanation for that. You might even want to know why I didn't include more photos from places like Indiana, Canada, Alabama or Missouri? The answer is simple. The vast majority of the surviving stereoviews and glass-negative photos we see today were taken in specific areas: namely Maine and parts of New England, the Adirondacks of New York and the upper Midwest. There are two reasons for this trend. These areas represented the epicenter of deer hunting activity in America 100 years ago, and as a result, this is where the majority of photos were made. I have tried very hard to include photos from other areas but they are simply not as easy to find as those taken in the regions mentioned.

The purpose of this book is to chronicle some of the rich history and heritage of whitetail hunting across North America as it was recorded on photographs in many parts of the country during the late 1800s and early 1900s. My hope is that the book will offer a unique glimpse into a rich bygone era. Most of the photos have never been published and they depict a wide variety of deer hunting activities. Many were taken at a time when there were no closed seasons or bag limits. That's why so many of the old photos show deer camps with dozens of deer including does, fawns and bucks hanging on the meat pole. This was an important time in the evolution of deer hunting in America because it was when whitetail hunting became an American institution for individuals, groups of friends, families and ethnic groups from a variety of European backgrounds.

Most hunters love to pore over photos of other hunters posed with their trophies in magazines, books and even on cell phones and computers. Most of us just can't resist old vintage photos. It's important to remember the past and learn from it, and deer hunters have an inherent curiosity about the golden days of yesteryear. In a way, a classic vintage photo is like a time machine, and when we hunters look back in time, we often see ourselves in the pictures. Even if we can't be that person, we can imagine and fantasize about how things were in the old days.

The photo of young Noel Thompson is a great example. Here is a beaming young farm boy from Washington state in the prime of life with his Savage Model 99, holding up a rack that he is obviously very proud of. This is one of my favorite pictures in the entire book. What I'd give to go back 100 years and meet young Noel in person!

There is a real magic and fascination in going back in time and looking at people who were doing the same thing we have such a passion for doing today. When we do, we quickly come to the realization that these people were amazingly plugged in to what they were doing without access to all of the high-tech aids available in the 21st century. Although there were no cell phones, no GPS, no trail cameras, no treestands, no Outdoor Channel, no Realtree camouflage and in many areas – no hunting allowed on Sunday, we form a bond with these old-time hunters because we come to realize that deer hunting really hasn't changed all that much. We still battle the same cold, the wind, the elements and we still get buck fever. In a way, we are an incarnation of those who came before us.

This book was a labor of love. I will forever be indebted to my editor Chris Berens for believing in this project and making it happen. I hope you enjoy looking at the photos as much as I enjoyed researching them and writing about them. Whitetails are American originals, and whitetail hunting is a uniquely American tradition. No other country in the world can claim what we have. Whitetails contributed immensely toward the building of this country. The mingled destinies of whitetails and men in America long ago became an extraordinary partnership that has lasted for nearly 400 years. The story is far from being complete. Many more chapters will be written in the future. Maybe there should be a national holiday or day of recognition dedicated to these amazing creatures. God bless America, God bless whitetail hunters everywhere and God bless America's deer. May the next century of whitetail hunting be as rich and fruitful as the last.

"America grew up eating venison and wearing buckskin.

"We were weaned as a nation on deer meat, took our first toddling steps in deerhide moccasins, and came of age at King's Mountain and New Orleans when our deer-trained riflemen cut down foreign regulars in long scarlet swaths.

"We scraped, oiled and stretched buckskin over our cabin windows in lieu of glass. When the crops were put by, maybe we walked down the mountain to a turnpike or tavern and swapped deer hides for the venomous rum we called 'The Crown's Revenge.' In early Kaintuck when there was no flour we gave our babies boiled venison instead of bread. Moving west, we spliced the first telegraph lines with buckskin thongs and tipped our 30-foot bullwhips with buckskin poppers. We dressed our heroes in buckskin, gloves and mukluks, and sent them off to Lundy's Lane, the Alamo, the Little Big Horn, Attu and Aachen.

"And we're still people of the deer. A pair of wealthy Detroit executives, lunching at their club, grin like boys as they plan the fall deer hunt. A Carolina mountain farmer, waking to find frost in the laurel thickets, oils the lock of his ten-pound 'hawg rifle' and winks at his son.

"Anyone from the outcountry knows that a proper man looks first to his Bible, then to his buck rifle, and then to the business of deer. These things done, he has put himself in proper order to look after his nation."

John Madson, 1961
From *The White-Tailed Deer*, published by the Conservation Department of Olin Mathieson Chemical Company, East Alton, Illinois.

CHAPTER 1

PIONEERS & NEW FRONTIERS

The Civil War brought death and destruction, misery and defeat to the people and the land in many areas east of the Rocky Mountains, particularly in the South. But as wars always do, those four ugly years also brought worlds of new technology. Geniuses like John Moses Browning (1855-1926) emerged to bring forth a totally new generation of arms that quickly found their way into the deer woods. On the western plains the new repeating rifles were used by the Indians to fight the soldiers who wanted to put them on reservations, and by the soldiers who wanted to do away with the Indians altogether. While the men of the eastern forests quickly realized that the Henry and Winchester repeaters were great innovations for deer, bear and moose hunting.

Before 1876 when Custer went down in a senseless blaze of glory, someone might have warned him that the Indians he was fighting outgunned him by a substantial margin. Many of the Sioux and Cheyenne warriors at the Little Big Horn were armed with state-of-the-art Henry and Winchester repeaters – and they knew how to use them. But, typical of the postwar, cost-conscious U.S. Army that always seemed to be behind the times, Custer's soldiers were armed with awkward single-shot Springfield trapdoor carbines left over from Civil War days.

Eastern hunters, having chased deer for generations with old percussion muzzleloaders that had been converted from flintlocks and passed down from father to son, quickly discovered that the new rifles of the 1870s, '80s and '90s were more accurate, faster handling and had more firepower behind those newfangled centerfire bullets being launched at wily bucks.

After the Civil War, the tens of thousands of men who had served as soldiers and sacrificed so much simply wanted to go home, farm their land or eke out a living doing other jobs in peace and harmony in the small communities from which they had come. The Gilded Age of the late 1800s brought an industrial revolution to the cities, but the common man still toiled long hours and little time was available for much else other than backbreaking work. On those rare occasions when a man and his sons or companions might slip away for a few days and seek the solitude and beauty of the wilderness, deer hunting became an almost sacred form of recreation for people rich and poor from all walks of life. It served a number of purposes.

First, it provided delicious meat for the table and helped subsidize the food bill during hard times. Second, since many folks were born with that primordial inner need and desire to get out in nature and hunt like their ancestors had done thousands of years earlier, no game animal in the world was more destined or better suited to fill that need than the widely distributed white-tailed deer.

Lastly, even though there were numerous challenges and a hunter often had to fight some very tough and unforgiving elements to achieve his desired result, deer hunting was a very satisfying and rewarding avocation. It gave each hunter a deep sense of worth and built strong character.

In addition to the abundance of new and innovative firearms, photography emerged as a new medium during the Civil War with which to permanently record historic events. From the mid-1870s into the early 20th century, innovations in photography continued to advance. Literally tens of thousands of photographs were taken depicting every facet of one of America's favorite pastimes – hunting elusive whitetails. The daguerreotypes and tintypes of the mid-1800s gave way to large format glass negatives

and finally film in the early 1900s. Stereoviews, cabinet photos and photo postcards became enormously popular, and many of the surviving photos we see today depict priceless deer hunting scenes from yesteryear.

When you study these old photos, you have to ask: Have things really changed all that much? Certainly the deer we hunt today are the same animals our forefathers hunted a century ago, and the people who hunt today are filled with the same emotions. We still miss shots, we still get afflicted with buck fever, and we still love to sit around the campfire at night and tell half-true yarns about the ones that got away.

Yes, technology has made it much easier for us today, but getting up a 4 a.m. and watching the sun rise as you wait for that elusive buck to appear on a cold November morning will always be a gift. Going back in time to see how our grandfathers and great grandfathers did it 100 years ago is also a gift.

4998. Weary and Hungry, but HAPPY.

⌃ CONTEMPLATING HIS PRIZE

This bearded old-timer could easily be a Civil War veteran. He is perfectly content as he sits on the edge of the creek reflecting about yet another successful hunt. After a good morning's tramp in the snow and a few moments of rest, it'll soon be time to get this deer back to the camp. With a long-barrel Pennsylvania rifle, an Arkansas toothpick and an old Smith & Wesson revolver in his belt, this skilled hunter is ready for any challenge that Mother Nature might throw at him. Titled "Weary and Hungry, but Happy," the stereoview by B.W. Kilburn was registered in 1888. The photo was taken in New England, likely New Hampshire or Vermont.

◁ LET THE FEAST BEGIN

A lucky New England family will enjoy some fine eating tonight. This very early stereoview, taken in the late 1860s or early 1870s, bearing the caption "Winter Sports," depicts a well-used pair of snowshoes and two very old pre-Civil War percussion-cap muzzleloaders – one a double shotgun and the other a rifle. The results of an exceptionally good day afield are also portrayed: a fine young buck, several snowshoe hares, and several "partridges," or ruffed grouse.

This stereoview was also photographed and published by the Kilburn Brothers of Littleton, N.H., and comes from a series taken in New Hampshire's rugged and scenic White Mountains. Once a remote wilderness, today much of the area is contained in public land. The Appalachian Trail crosses the White Mountains in New Hampshire from southwest to northeast.

2198. Discussing the Shot

▲ A GOOD DAY IN THE WOODS

A snowshoe hare and a yearling doe are depicted in this 1876 stereoview titled "Discussing the Shot." The man standing is holding a percussion shotgun while his kneeling partner is brandishing an extremely long-barrel Pennsylvania rifle. Note the curved powder horn hanging around his waist. This photo comes from "The Leather-stocking Series," published by the Kilburn Brothers in Littleton, N.H., a series designed to "illustrate the most exciting and fascinating moments in the Hunter's experience." Ironically, this photo was taken only a few months after George Armstrong Custer and his men tragically made national headlines in June 1876, having been overwhelmed by superior numbers at the Battle of the Little Big Horn in Montana.

⌄ "GEMS OF THE ADIRONDACKS"

This classic deer camp photo taken in the 1875, about 10 years after the Civil War, could almost be a Matthew Brady photo of a Civil War-era encampment. Instead, these rugged hunters, some of whom could well be Yankee veterans, are gathered in a late-summer deer camp in the Adirondacks as evidenced by the velvet buck hanging in the foreground. Few if any game laws existed in the Adirondacks in those days.

From an early stereoview titled "Fall River Camp, Roland Pond," the photo was taken by Baldwin Photo of Keeseville, N.Y. Written on the front of the decorated stereoview are the words: "Gems of the Adirondacks." The men are believed to be local Saranac Lake guides who worked out of nearby Rustic, Martin's or Bartlett's Lodges, all popular hunting lodges of that time that catered to wealthy New Yorkers and Bostonians. Of particular interest are the men's rifles. At least one Henry repeater and two Martini-Henry single-shot breechloading rifles appear in the photo. One hunter sitting by the flap of the tent ap-

pears to be holding a muzzleloading shotgun.

The Martini-Henry lever-action breechloader was a single-shot rifle that was developed in Europe in the early 1870s. It chambered a large, .450-caliber bullet that weighed 485 grains. Known for its tremendous knockdown power, the brass bottlenecked bullet was similar to the American .45-70.

The Martini-Henry became quite popular for big-game hunting in Africa in the late 1800s. During the famous Zulu wars in South Africa, British troops were armed with this rifle on Jan. 23, 1879, during the ill-fated Battle of Isandlwanda in which the British suffered an overwhelming defeat. Outnumbered by an estimated 50 to 1, the British regiment was nearly wiped out by Zulu warriors using mostly spears and shields that were led by the famous Shaka Zulu.

Today, much of the land surrounding Roland Pond in upstate New York is a state park with public campgrounds. Truly, this stereoview is a "gem" of a bygone time.

"NO, IT WAS MY LOAD OF 00 BUCK THAT BROUGHT HIM DOWN!"

We often hear the phrase, "one good picture is worth a thousand words." As modern-day deer hunters, we are truly blessed to have so many old photos that help us visually preserve the past. But wouldn't it be nice if we could also listen in on some of the rich conversations that took place in thousands of deer camps located in thousands of different locations across this great country a century ago? While that may not be possible, we can use our imagination to guess at what these excited hunters might be saying. Are they arguing about who actually shot the deer? Are they reliving the day's hunt? Could the animated hunter pointing to the deer be saying, "No, it was my load of 00 buck that brought him down!"

Since three of these men are armed with rabbit-ear shotguns (the gun on the porch actually appears to be a flintlock rifle or shotgun), the buck and doe pictured were probably taken during an organized deer drive. The man on the far right is holding an 1876 Winchester lever-action rifle, and the man next to him has a newfangled Martini-Henry breechloading single-shot rifle. Photo circa late 1880s.

HOLDING COURT

Although no location is given in this 1890 stereoview published by B.W. Kilburn of Littleton, N.H., it may well be somewhere in the Adirondacks. Titled "Our Christmas Hunt, story at the Camp," the gentlemen hunters are discussing the morning's outing in front of their log shack. It's interesting to note the camp's sign above the very low doorway just behind the hunters.

The man on the right has a fancy muzzleloading shotgun, while the well-dressed man in the center of the group has a saddle-ring Winchester carbine. The quaint rifle held by the man on the left is a unique skeleton or bicycle rifle, probably in .22 caliber, used for small game like squirrels and rabbits.

5329. Our Christmas Hunt, story at the Camp.

A WAGON FULL OF VENISON

With a pile of antlered bucks in the bed of this extra-long wagon, one has to wonder if these men are market hunters or sport hunters from a Northwoods deer camp. Most likely they are market hunters taking the spoils of their hunt into town to sell. The photo was taken in northern Wisconsin or Minnesota. Judging by the huge stumps in the background, the virgin timber was removed from the area several years earlier. Photo circa late 1800s.

THE BOYS ARE BACK IN THE WOODS

This faded cabinet photo tells a timeless story. Withstanding the elements in a deep, fresh snow and loving every minute of it, this group of stalwart hunters has achieved its goal. The eager young boy in the middle holding the shotgun is very symbolic. His father, perhaps the man standing next to him, is doing his part in passing on a great America tradition.

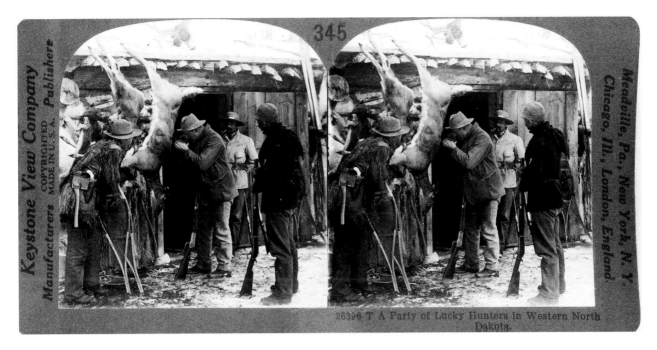

⌃ A PARTY OF LUCKY HUNTERS IN WESTERN NORTH DAKOTA

These seasoned hunters are decked out with all the trappings of the chase; snowshoes, wooden skis, classic rifles of the day, axes, pistols – everything they need to ply their trade in the rugged badlands of North Dakota. Their Winchester rifles have spoken, and now these men can pause for a moment, light their pipes and relive the highlights of the day. In a wild and rugged country made famous by future president Theodore Roosevelt in the mid-1880s, the river bottoms and badlands of western North Dakota claim both whitetails and mule deer. The deer hanging in the middle is a whitetail doe, while the deer hanging just behind is a mule deer. Note the mule deer rack on the roof of the cabin.

One of the most popular rifles of the day, a Winchester Model 1876 is held by the hunter on the right. At least one of the rifles leaning against the cabin also appears to be a trusty '76. The man in the middle lighting his pipe is leaning against a revolutionary new Winchester Model 94. Who could have guessed in the late 1890s that millions of these rifles would be sold to deer hunters in the decades ahead? Stereoview circa late 1800s.

⌃ A FINE DAY'S BOUNTY

A quaint farm somewhere in the Northeast, on a misty November afternoon sets the stage for a successful day's hunt as this group of older gentlemen pose with a respectable day's bounty. The men are holding a variety of rifles and shotguns. The short, white-bearded gentleman on the right could well be a survivor of Gettysburg and other Civil War engagements. Earlier in the day, these men may have conducted several organized drives that resulted in this fine array of venison on the hoof. Photo circa 1900.

NOW THAT'S A HEALTHY SPIKE!

This mustached gentleman wearing snow gaiters is "ready for bear" as he poses with his winter's supply of venison – a large bodied spikehorn buck – in mountainous country very reminiscent of the northeast; northern Maine or the Adirondacks. He is holding a John Browning designed, long-barrel Winchester Model 1894 with a half magazine. Mr. Browning hit a home run with this popular repeater. Photo circa late 1890s.

A LUCKY DAY

With knife in hand, a hunter examines a beautiful 8-point buck as his partner, toting a hefty doe, looks on. From an Underwood & Underwood Publishers 1901 stereoview titled "A lucky day on the Oak Ridges, Indian Territory, U.S.A." In 1901, Indian Territory U.S.A. included most of the state of Oklahoma. We can't be sure where the "oak ridges" were located, but wherever these two adventurers were plying their trade that day, the whitetail hunting was superb and memorable.

This old cabinet photo depicts three well-dressed men standing next to several bucks and does hanging in front of a picket fence, along with several other carcasses behind them including a plucked turkey and a couple of rabbits. The photo is marked: "Gravely and Moore, Charleston." Benjamin Frank Gravely Sr. was a well-known photographer in Charleston, W.Va., who began taking photos around 1860. His son later opened a studio under the name of Gravely and Moore around 1902. It's likely this photo was made by the senior Gravely from a glass negative in the 1880s or early 1890s.

➤ TAR HEEL TROPHY

(1) Cradling his Winchester lever action, most likely a Model 1892 or '94, over his arm while carrying a fine 8-point buck through the vast piney wood flatlands of eastern North Carolina, this Tar Heel hunter heads back to camp to rendezvous with his companions and divide his bounty equally among friends.

(2) Everyone takes part in the cleaning chore. The cigar-smoking man standing on the left may be holding the fresh liver, while the man kneeling is removing the entrails. Our hero holds the deer up while two white-bearded old-timers, who could easily be Civil War veterans, supervise the procedure.

Throughout the 1800s, the tar, pitch and turpentine from the endless pine forests of eastern North Carolina were crucial to the state's economy. The term "Tar Heel" seems to have derived its roots from that enterprise. After the Civil War, the term was often used as a slur much like the term redneck or hillbilly. Today, North Carolinians wear the name with pride. Photos circa 1900.

THE HUNTER'S RETURN – RESULT OF THE CHASE

Written on the back of this stereoview:

"To the lover of the chase, the scene here presented is one of great interest. It suggests to his fancy thrilling adventures and hot pursuits over hills and valleys, through underbrush and forest streams. It recalled the crackle of the camp-fire and the odor of the boiling camp-kettle which promises a savory repast; the jolly good fellowship of comrades around the ruddy blaze, the interchange of hunter's yarns and then the sweet repose on mattresses of evergreen boughs after the day's weary tramp.

"The hunters who have spent many days in the forests of Maine, miles from human habitation, have broken camp, and returned with their quarry to the hotel from which they started, and are viewing with apparent satisfaction the result of the week's chase. An immense moose and several fine deer make up the capture. On the sled may be seen the head and the hide of a deer which was used as venison while in camp. The head is regarded as one of rare beauty by huntsmen who are competent judges.

"This picture was taken in Ashland, Me, Dec. 5th, 1898."

From Keystone View Company, Meadville, Pa., and St. Louis, Mo.

SQUIRREL STEW TONIGHT, BOYS

The old gentleman on the left is de-furring a squirrel that will no doubt go into the pot while his younger partner begins to field dress a large doe. The unusual shotgun leaning against the tree is a Spencer pump action, probably in 12-gauge. Produced by the Spencer Arms Co. in Connecticut between 1882 and 1889, this was the first commercially successful slide-action pump shotgun on the market. Most were manufactured in 12-gauge, but the gun was also available in 10-gauge. The company was bought out in 1890 by Francis Bannerman & Sons who continued to manufacture the popular shotgun into the early 1900s.

LIVING IN THE LAP OF LUXURY

Talk about roughing it. You can almost smell the aroma of hot black coffee and stew sizzling in the pot as this veteran woodsman prepares some grub in his primitive camp. His Winchester Model 1887 lever-action shotgun has spoken, and a fine yearling buck has been accounted for, intentionally hung high off the ground to keep the critters away. With all the comforts of home, this grizzled old pioneer whitetail hunter seems quite content. Life is good!

Taken in New England in the late 1800s, the stereoview was published in 1901 by Underwood & Underwood. The caption under the photo reads: "Old Hunter, cozy Camp in a log."

The gargantuan hardwood log had definitely been sawed, indicating that the tree was cut during the era of logging virgin timber in the late 1800s. It was probably left on the ground intentionally because it had heart rot, hence the hollowed-out area that will keep man and beast alike dry, warm and cozy in the worst of weather.

A RARE BREED OF WHITETAILS

Three rugged characters brandishing Marlin and Winchester lever-action rifles pose for the camera as a fourth and older man sitting in a chair looks on. In a photo postcard postmarked April 1903, one of the young men with the initials L.O. writes: "A picture taken near Mist after today's hunt. Your wumble (sp) servant killed the one with the horns."

Mist, Ore., is located in the extreme northwest portion of the state. The three whitetails pictured are of the subspecies Columbian whitetails. They are the westernmost subspecies of whitetails found in the U.S. Columbian whitetails once ranged along the Pacific coast of Oregon and Washington. But overhunting and poaching nearly exterminated them. By the early 1900s when this photo was taken, they were becoming extremely rare. Hunting for them was banned in the mid-20th century and they were placed on the endangered species list in 1968. Today they are making a strong comeback, thanks to the good conservation measures that have protected them for nearly 50 years.

DAYS GONE BY
A WEEK IN DEER CAMP

The North Country, Late 1800s
(Photos made from glass negatives, circa 1890.)

fighting off the chill of early morning. When the time comes to climb out from under warm blankets in the predawn darkness, hurriedly get dressed, eat a hardy breakfast and head to a favorite stand, the stove will be worth its weight in gold. Rugged living, yes, but a week's worth of living in a remote deer camp will no doubt render a lifetime of cherished memories. Speaking of making memories, what will the morning yield? Will some lucky hunter in the group bring back the buck of his dreams?

3. DRESSING FOR THE OCCASION
No, they're not going to a Sunday camp meeting. This is the way men dressed for deer camp in the late 1800s. With their vests, jackets, gold pocket watches and other finery, the well-dressed camp elders have one of the young hunters performing the heavy lifting for the group. Perhaps the road is being cleared of fallen trees and stones to make it passable for a horse-drawn wagon or sled.

4. FIRST BLOOD
The ever-reliable Marlin 1893 lever-action .38-55 has spoken and fresh backstraps aplenty will be sizzling on the stove tonight. As is often the case, it looks like the youngest hunters in camp have been the first to draw blood. Judging by the looks on their faces, these two young men could not be more proud of their bounty. Even though this 6-month-old doe will provide some savory camp vittles, there is still plenty of time for these eager young woodsmen to return and search out that elusive monarch of the North – especially after that first good tracking snow of the season arrives. The young man in the back is toting a Winchester Model 1894 while his partner in the front is carrying a trusty Marlin.

1. LAKE SCENE
Somewhere in the wilderness a large lake begins to freeze over. Deer camp beckons. From the looks of the terrain and lake, the scene is reminiscent of the Adirondacks in upstate New York. Once virgin trees, towering nearly 100 feet above the earth with girths so thick that a man couldn't reach around them, are noticeably absent from the forest. The area was logged only a few years earlier. Inadvertently, man's endless quest for wood to build an ever-expanding nation has one positive side effect. Thousands of acres of semi-open habitat and edge cover have been transformed – creating prime whitetail habitat.

2. HOME-SWEET-HOME FOR A WEEK
Two rugged wall tents, one with a tall smokestack for the wood-burning stove inside that will be used for cooking and

5. A LABOR OF LOVE

With knife in hand and a small hand ax strapped over his shoulder, this young hunter looks like he knows what he's doing, and he's more than ready to tackle the job so that he can prove to all of the camp elders that he is a genuine deer hunter. Beside him rests his trusty Marlin 1893 lever gun.

6. SHOTGUN MAN

No one is idle in deer camp for long. There is much work to be done, even for the camp elders. It takes a constant supply of wood to keep the fires burning and to insure that those cold nights are made a little more bearable inside the canvas. But what has interrupted this old gentleman's wood-cutting chore? Did he suddenly eye a grouse or a squirrel while splitting wood? Or is he just having some fun and posing with his old pump shotgun? If so, do you think he ever imagined that fellow deer hunters would be viewing his mug shot over a century later in a book dedicated to preserving the golden days of whitetail hunting? Thanks to one enterprising camp member with a newfangled Kodak, a record of this historic time will live for years to come.

7. OLD WHITEY IS DOWN

While three men pull the wooden sled holding this wide-spreading bull-of-the-woods, two others carry their rifles and admire the spoils of the day. What a buck! A massive 10-pointer with a rocking chair rack! Is this the legendary buck everyone in camp has been chasing, the phantom of the forest? How did he meet his demise? Was he following a doe on this cold and snowy day? Which of the men is the lucky hunter who did the deed?

Perhaps the men all took stands in the woods earlier in the morning, trail watching, full of expectation and hope. Perhaps some or all of them opted to maneuver a deer drive, or even follow a set of fresh tracks in the snow. Whatever the case may have been on that unforgettable day 120 years ago, the silence of the morning was broken with a piercing shot. Everyone knew that one lucky soul in the group had connected. Now each man gladly pitches in to help get this big boy back to camp. Thank goodness the lake is frozen over.

8. A SAGGING BUCK POLE TELLS THE TALE

The week is not even over yet and five big northern bucks, including Old Whitey on the end, hang proudly for all to see. A few smaller hindquarters from partially butchered does share the sagging pole, producing plenty of contented smiles. With this much venison, you know it's been another extraordinary week in deer camp.

A TROPHY PIEBALD

Hunters have always been fascinated with piebald deer and these two Adirondack deerslayers have taken a whopper. Both men are hunting with Winchester lever-action rifles, one a short carbine, the other a full-length rifle. This beautiful and unique deer no doubt created quite a bit of excitement back at camp; not only for its large rack but also for its unusual markings. Adirondack Mountains, 1915.

"As a trophy the whitetail leaves nothing to be desired. Cannily outwitting all but the best (and luckiest) of hunters – many times, it seems, by divine guidance – when finally taken he should be highly prized. His dark red flesh is a table delicacy when properly handled and prepared; his tough, pliable hide makes the softest of gloves and outer garments; the head, with its neat antlers, becomes a favorite decoration for the hunter's den."

Lawrence R. Koller
Shots at Whitetails, 1948

CHAPTER 2

TRAMPING IN THE ADIRONDACKS

Tramping in the Adirondacks – that is, hunting America's deer, the whitetail, fishing for trout, canoeing, exploring and enjoying nature, camping and living off the land for days at a time – is a purely American tradition that began back in the early 1800s. In his classic book, *Hunting Adventures in the Northern Wilds; or A Tramp in the Chateaugay Woods, Over Hills, Lakes, and Forest Streams*, published in 1856, S. H. Hammond paints a vivid picture of the outdoor life in the Adirondack wilderness during the first half of the 19th century.

In the book's dedication Hammond quotes:
"To follow the stag, o'er the slippery crag, And chase the bounding roe"

Of course, these were European terms borrowed from those brave souls who came to the New World with a new set of ideals. Hunting stags in England was as old as history itself, although in the Old World only the gentry and royalty enjoyed the privilege. If the common man were going to hunt rabbits and deer to help feed his family, he did it at the risk of life and limb.

European traditions such as hunting "stags" with packs of hounds were brought to America and copied to some extent. But, those die-hard people who began calling themselves Americans soon developed their very own styles and rituals for hunting an extraordinary and unique game animal that was native only to the North American continent. This incredible animal fed, clothed and even helped earn a living for many people who struggled to survive in the New World. Later, when it was no longer necessary for pioneers and settlers to hunt solely for food and clothing, this challenging animal became the most popular big-game animal in the history of the world.

In Hammond's day, a tramp in the Adirondacks meant traveling in a virtual wilderness filled with lakes, mountains and streams where few whites had ever dared to tread. A man could catch his own breakfast and dinner in a lake or stream, or feed on a ham from a deer recently shot. At night, he would sleep under the stars by a warm fire and listen to the sounds of the loon, the whippoorwill, or perhaps a lonely bobcat looking for a mate. The next day he might run into native Indians who were usually friendly and curious. Every day was a new adventure amidst a scenic wonderland of beauty and splendor.

During the mid-1800s, wealthy businessmen from New York, Boston and other eastern population centers founded numerous lodges in the Adirondacks. Men from the big cities of the Northeast had a yearning to get away from civilization and spend a few glorious days hunting for heavy old mossback bucks or fishing for native brook trout. That purely American ritual has continued right up to the present time. Local guides were hired to help find game and assist with the camp chores.

The latter half of the 19th century saw an increase in the number of people traveling to the Adirondacks for outdoor recreation. Rail transportation made the region much more accessible. Today, many of the lodges in the Adirondacks draw vacationers who enjoy a wide variety of outdoor pursuits – in addition to deer hunting.

Obviously the American scene has changed quite a bit in the past two centuries, but some things will never change. The rugged Adirondacks, in all of their magnificence, along with that American original, the noble white-tailed deer, still lure countless thousands of hunters each year who tramp the mountains in search of a trophy. Lodges and hunting camps are still filled to capacity during hunting season.

The word "tramp" has several definitions in the dictionary: "to walk with a firm heavy step," "to traverse on foot," or "one who travels aimlessly about as a vagrant." I'm sure S.H. Hammond would have gotten a big kick out of being called a vagrant as he explored his beloved Chateaugay woods and caught trout on every cast from a serene lake 175 years ago. Like the deer he chased and the woods he traversed, the word "tramping" seems to be an American original. At least it has a good, old-fashioned "American" ring to it.

Season after season, decade after decade, for well over 200 years, men have made an annual pilgrimage to the sacred mountains in New York to rediscover themselves and seek solace and recreation amidst the breathtaking setting. In many ways, the deer camps of yesteryear are not unlike those of today. Thank goodness there are so many similarities.

⋀ LIVING A DREAM

In the wilds of the Adirondacks, this exhilarated but weary sportsman dozes in the front of the canoe with his 1876 Winchester lever action across his lap as the guide lazily paddles back to camp across a still and serene lake. Every few minutes, the hunter opens his eyes – just to make sure his impressive and eye-catching 10-point trophy whitetail is actually in the canoe with him, as if to say, "Please pinch me to make sure this is not a dream!" Note the guide's dog along for the ride. Photo circa 1877.

END OF THE HUNT

Another memorable wilderness hunt has come to an end, and the time has come to stow the Adirondack baskets and other gear and head back across the lake toward civilization. The hunting has been good as evidenced by the antlers prominently showing in the first boat. The men in the back of each of the four bateaus are probably guides, while the "sports" or hunters wait on the shore to assist the loading. Photo circa 1910.

String of Deer at Elk Lake 1907.

James Leach, at Elk Lake, N.Y. 1907.

ELK LAKE DREAM BUCK

Mr. James Leach, a well-dressed and debonaire "gentleman" hunter, poses in suit and tie with an outstanding, heavy beamed 10-point buck, a large doe and a yearling doe taken in the woods around Elk Lake in the heart of the Adirondacks. Mr. Leach was probably a well-to-do business-man from New York or Boston who traveled to the Adirondacks each year to "tramp the mountains" and hunt whitetails with friends and business associates. Once a remote wilderness, Elk Lake has been a popular re-sort destination for many decades.

▲ **ADIRONDACKS CAMP HOUSE 1890s**

   Rustic at best, a typical Adirondacks camp house in the late 1800s could accommodate up to 20 hunters. At the end of a long day in the woods, deer camp wouldn't be deer camp without a spirited game of poker in the evening. After a successful day in the woods, the men are loading a couple of big bucks brought in on boats onto horse-drawn sleds that will take them to camp. Numerous lakes dot the Adirondacks region and hunters often used boats to reach prime hunting spots.

▲ THE PRIDE OF
THE ADIRONDACKS

"The Pride of the Adirondacks" may be an understatement. With a picturesque lakefront setting, a small boathouse and boat, a cabin to the right and five fine deer hanging, is there anything truly closer to heaven on earth than this? Photo circa 1920s.

Deer
HUNTING

ILLUSTRATED

FRANK A. KURANT *Author*

Illustrations By HAROLD BLITTERSDORF

> ROUGHING IT

The smiles say it all! Based on the number of New York Conservation Department hunting license pins they are wearing on their hats, this jovial group is headed into the wilds of the Adirondacks for a few days of camaraderie and tramping in one of the nation's most scenic areas. Although they appear ready for bear, they will be hunting America's most challenging big-game animal.

Note the Adirondack baskets they are wearing that carry all of their vital gear and food. The hunter nearest to the camera is armed with a Remington Model 8. Leaning against the log next to that is a Savage 99, obviously belonging to the man taking the photo. The glass jug is a mystery. What could be inside? Is it maple syrup for the pancakes or could it be a jug of heart attack medicine? Photo circa 1930s.

GAME LAWS OF NEW YORK AND WISCONSIN.
DEER.

NEW YORK.—There is no open season for moose, elk, caribou or antelope. As they were long since exterminated the only purpose the law serves now is to protect such as are introduced for breeding purposes. Common deer may be hunted from September 1 to November 16. No person may take more than two in a season. Fawns in the spotted or red coat may not be taken at any time. Hunting with dogs, traps, salt licks or other device is prohibited. Penalties for violation are as high as $350 fine and one year's imprisonment.— Revised Statutes to 1901.

FROM A STEREOVIEW BY KEYSTONE VIEW COMPANY DATED 1901.

▲ ADIRONDACK HEAVYWEIGHT

With a pipe in hand and a trusty Winchester stretched across his impressive trophy, Donald Otis of St. Hubert's, N.Y., poses with one of several outstanding Adirondacks ridge runners he brought down in the 1940s and '50s. Judging from the heavy rack on this big-bodied mountain buck, the old boy might have been on the decline. With exceptional mass and a right G-2 that looks to be at least 12 inches long, he would be considered a "dream buck" to most hunters in the Adirondacks today. To Donald, it was just an average buck.

"No one at the time considered the buck in the photo to be of any great significance," remembers Brian Straight of Au Sable Forks, N.Y., Donald's grandson. "It was just another nice buck that made the mistake of stepping out

in front of my grandfather who was an amazing shot. My grandfather had two 14-point bucks that had been mounted and hung on his porch wall. He shot them a year apart and their racks were so close to being identical that he called them his 'twins.' Either of them might have made the record book had he bothered to have them scored."

The rifle is a classic, long-barrel Winchester lever action.

"Pretty rare I was told," Brian said. "It was my grandfather's favorite deer rifle."

Winchester offered a variety if calibers in the early 1900s including the .25-35 WCF, the .30 WCF and the .38-55. Of course, the .30-30 was by far the most popular round in the 1930s and '40s with the .32 Winchester Special running a distant second. Photo courtesy of Brian Straight.

THE CHAMPION BUCK KILLER
OF THE HOLLYWOOD CLUB

At a time when few women hunted with their husbands, Peg Smith was a true pioneer in her own right. Her husband, Nick Smith, had joined the legendary hunting club known as the Hollywood Club in Essex County, N.Y., in 1938. Today in its seventh generation, the Hollywood Club is one of New York state's oldest hunting clubs. The club was founded in the mid-1880s by several businessmen from Boston, New York and New Jersey who loved to hunt and fish in the Adirondacks.

At the outbreak of World War II, Nick, along with millions of other young men, went off to fight for his country. Nick joined the Marines and was shipped to the Pacific. Very little hunting took place on the club property during the war years for obvious reasons. But all of that changed in the fall of 1945. The war had just ended on September 2 with the surrender of Japan. It must have been a jubilant time for Nick and Peg, and the first thing they did was plan a fall hunt together at the Hollywood Club.

During its early years, the Hollywood Club was strictly a "men's only" club. Eventually, however, the "no women allowed" rule was relaxed. In 1945, the Adirondack deer season ran from Oct. 20 to Nov. 30 with a one buck limit. Nick and Peg participated in the club-wide October hunt without filling their buck tags. By now, they had become very good friends with club members George Perkins and his wife Dot. The foursome frequently hunted and socialized together. Undaunted by their lack of opening-day luck, they decided to go back to the club property and hunt the final few days of the season in late November.

Peg's half-Indian guide Roland Ferry described her hunt as follows: "Me and Mrs. Nick were tramping along quiet out west of the camp near the big swamp when I seen a big deer's body in a bunch of small spruce. We stopped, and soon I seen the head come up with a gosh-awful bunch of horns on top, I whispers to Mrs. Nick, 'Shoot! It's an elephant!' 'Are you sure it's a buck?' says she. 'Cripes, yes! Shoot!' says I. She ups with the rifle (an open-sighted Winchester lever-action .30-30 carbine), whangs away, and down drops the buck. We went up to him and he had the dangdest set of horns I ever seen. She was pretty excited, of course, and the first thing I knew she busted out bawling. 'What the hell's the matter?' I says. 'Look,' she says, 'look! I killed him when he was just eating his breakfast.' There were some pieces of fern sticking out of his mouth, which gave her the idea, but the weeps didn't last long with that big walloper lyin' there, the first buck she had ever seen and bagged so slick."

Peg Smith was soon lauded and regaled as the cham-

pion buck killer of the Hollywood Club. Her impressive 6-by-6 trophy was said to be the largest buck ever taken on the Hollywood Club property. In May 2004, after nearly a half-century, Peg Smith's great 1945 Adirondack trophy was officially scored by Northeast Big Bucks Club regional director Carl Lieser. With an 18-inch inside spread and both main beams measuring just over 25 inches, Peg's vintage trophy tallied up a net typical score of 163-6/8 Boone and Crockett points.

To many of the club members, both old and new, she remains to this day "the champion buck killer of the Hollywood Club!"

ALL GOOD THINGS MUST COME TO AN END

At the end of every hunt comes a feeling of sadness, a deep sense of loss. No doubt this wilderness traveler, by the name of Rick Brady, is feeling those pangs of regret now as he sits at the depot holding his Winchester rifle and awaiting the train that will take him back to civilization and a world filled with noises, clutter and the mayhem that is so much a part of city life.

Only yesterday Rick and his companions were in their wilderness camp in the Adirondacks, with his pack loaded with food and camping gear far off the beaten path. For a few glorious days or a even a week, he and his fellow hunters knew only the solitude of nature in an incredible landscape of lakes and mountains, the joy of waking up to the chill of a frosty November morning, and heading out of camp before daylight each morning to search for an elusive whitetail buck. The hunting had been good.

The success Rick and his adventurous companions found during their tramp in the Adirondacks is one consolation that will be measured in rich lifetime memories and the considerable quantity of venison going home with them. LaFargeville is a hamlet in northern New York named after a Frenchman, located not far from the eastern shore of Lake Ontario near the Canadian border. Photo circa 1920.

> **Too few Easterners appreciate the north woods (the Adirondacks). Year after year sportsmen travel to distant hunting grounds spending time and money for indifferent shooting when almost at their door lies one of God's most beautiful forests.**
>
> **Roy Chapman Andrews, 1930**

DODGE BROTHERS
SPECIAL
TYPE-A SEDAN

The aristocrat of Dodge Brothers line of closed cars. Yet so dependably built is the Special Type-A Sedan that frequently you find it serving under conditions that would try the sturdiest open cars.

This amazing capacity for long life and hard work is recognized everywhere as the outstanding characteristic of Dodge Brothers product.

It is strikingly evidenced by the fact that more than **90%** of all the motor cars Dodge Brothers have built during the past eleven years are still in active service—a record which stands impressively alone in automobile history.

Ask your dealer about Dodge Brothers
New Credit-Purchase Plan

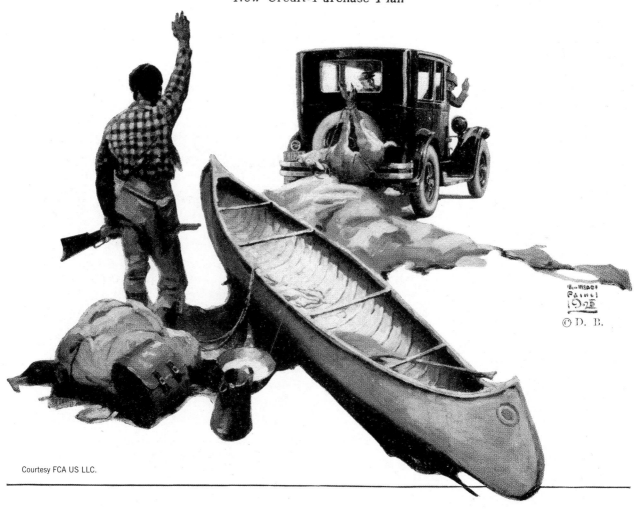

© D. B.

POSTCARDS FROM DEER CAMP

Printed postcards, both color and black and white, became quite popular across the Northeast in the early 1900s. Dozens of scenes depicting various facets of deer camp life in the Adirondacks were recorded on film for posterity. Many survive to this day, giving us a unique glimpse into the past.

≪ Postcard titled, "An Adirondack Hunting Scene, Adirondack Mountains, N.Y." Circa 1910.

⋏ A gentleman hunter and his bucks. Postcard titled, "With Canoe and Rifle in the North Woods." Circa 1910.

Postcard titled, "A Good Specimen of the Adirondack Deer, N.Y." Circa 1907.

A GOOD SPECIMEN OF THE   ADIRONDACK DEER. N.Y.

Getting ready for Supper
in a Typical Sporting Camp.

Postcard titled, "Getting Ready for Supper in a Typical Sporting Camp." Circa 1910.

Postcard titled, "Bringing Home the Spoils." Circa 1907.

A Winchester lever-action, an Adirondack basket and a fine New York buck. Lake Placid, Adirondacks, 1914.

Postcard titled, "Hunting in the Adirondacks, N.Y." Circa 1909.

A Tolerable Holdup: D. H. Come to 37 Wed. come early hoping you are better. S. B.

These Adirondack "sports" are enjoying their success. Postcard titled, "A Tolerable Holdup," circa 1905.

◁ Making the shot. Postcard titled, "Hunting Deer in the Adirondacks." Circa 1912.

◁ Postcard titled, "Adirondack Mts., N.Y. An Adirondack Camp." Circa 1908.

Adirondack Mts., N.Y. An Adirondack Camp.

An Adirondack Buck.

◁ Two hunters with their prize. Postcard titled, "An Adirondack Buck." Circa 1909.

AN ADIRONDACKS DEER CAMP

1950s

Has anything really changed? A century ago, men were doing the very same thing these "modern" deerslayers of the '50s arc doing in the very same rugged mountains. These men are from Manlius, N.Y., near Syracuse. Some, if not all, are members of the Manlius Volunteer Fire Department.

◅ Ready for bear! Another exciting deer hunting adventure begins as the cheerful hunters pack sleeping bags and other gear and prepare to hit the road for deer camp.

▽ Men catching some rest in their warm sleeping bags.

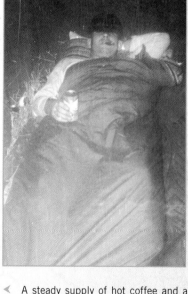

◅ A steady supply of hot coffee and a warm and dry place to rest your weary bones during the night, no matter how cold outside — these were the basic requirements needed to survive a week in the Adirondack wilderness in this mid-20th century camp. Anything beyond that was pure luxury. These innovative hunters have put down a thick layer of fresh straw inside their large wall tent for added comfort.

A large wall tent, probably Army surplus, that will easily sleep six to eight weary hunters and keep them dry and warm.

Washing up after breakfast.

Hanging the first trophy of the hunt – in this case a doe – on the meat pole. By the end of the week, the sturdy meat pole should be straining with hundreds of pounds of venison, including a couple of deer that will hopefully carry some bragging-size racks.

Breakfast is served!

By necessity, every wilderness deer camp has some sort of outside facility placed in a strategic location 40 or 50 yards downwind of camp. While some camps had very primitive arrangements, some of the more sophisticated camps went to great lengths to provide maximum comfort for their users.

SAVAGE LAND

   No Winchesters here. In a landscape dominated primarily by Winchester lever-action rifles and carbines, the hunter in this photo has a decided preference for his accurate Savage Model 99. What's more, the rifle has seen plenty of action in this Down East deer camp. The sturdy old log structures look reminiscent of a very old homesteader's spread, perhaps used as a deer camp by hunters in November. Photo circa 1920s.

> **You can hunt the world over for trophies-**
> **Far back of beyond you may go:**
> **But one day you'll come back,**
> **To follow the track,**
> **Of the whitetailed deer in the snow.**

William Monypeny Newsom
Whitetailed Deer, 1926

CHAPTER 3

DOWN EAST
THE BIG WOODS OF MAINE & THE NORTHEAST

Maine has long been regarded as a sportsman's paradise. Hunting, fishing and trapping have been outdoor pursuits practiced by passionate outdoorsmen for several hundred years. First used around 1825, the term "Down East" originally referred to the northern coastline of Maine. Over the years, the term was expanded to mean all of Maine, and eventually it came to represent much of the northeast section of the U.S. and parts of the Maritime Provinces of Canada.

In the first half of the 19th century, moose, deer and caribou were plentiful in northern Maine. By 1900, the caribou had been hunted down to the last animal. Several efforts throughout the 1900s to re-establish caribou in their native range around Mount Katahdin failed due to heavy poaching and predation. Moose were also overhunted, often for their thick hides. By 1935, moose hunting was banned altogether in an effort to re-establish a viable population. The season did not open again until 1980, when licenses were offered on a lottery basis. Whitetails, although hunted heavily for their hides and meat at times, never suffered the fate of moose and caribou.

An 1830 law set the annual hunting season for moose and deer from Sept. 1 through Dec. 31 with no bag limits. Much like the Adirondack region, Maine became a popular destination for wealthy out-of-state sportsmen in the mid-1800s. The expansion of the railroads to northern Maine in the late 1800s made the area much more accessible. Although nonresident hunters contributed a great deal to the local economies, the "gentlemen hunters" and "sports" from the big cities of the Northeast were greatly resented by resident hunters, especially those who made a living selling meat and hides. As a result, out-of-state hunters were banned from hunting in Maine from 1853 to 1870.

In 1883, a new law was passed that set the annual hunting season and bag limits for deer, moose and caribou from Oct. 1 to Jan. 1. Hunters could shoot one moose, two caribou and three deer. The new law also restricted hunting with dogs and banned Sunday hunting altogether – something that most other eastern states eventually adopted as well.

Around the turn of the century, concern over dwindling game populations prompted new efforts in conservation for both moose and deer. Sportsmen groups began to adopt new hunting behavior that was considered to be much more ethical than many of the old practices commonly used in the region. The longtime traditions of night hunting with "jack" lights, hunting with dogs, driving deer into lakes and other waterways where they could be easily dispatched, and shooting over the limit were considered unsportsmanlike practices that were greatly frowned upon.

The turn of the century also saw a surge in outfitting and a huge increase in sporting camps and licensed guides. Within a few decades, legendary hunters like Fred Goodwin and his brother Edwin ran successful deer camps for out-of-state "sports" in the 1930s, '40s and '50s.

The Winchester lever-action carbine quickly grew to be the rifle of choice in the Maine woods for deer, bear and moose. Produced locally by the Winchester Arms Company in New Haven, Conn., hunters across New England and eventually the entire country swore by this classic rifle. Around 1910, a brand-new Winchester Model 94 carbine could be ordered out of the Sears, Roebuck catalog for $16. A box of smokeless, centerfire .30-30 cartridges sold for under $1.

The golden days of whitetail hunting in the Northeast may be but a cherished memory, but the Big Woods of northern Maine still offer the avid whitetail hunter adventure, excitement and some of the most beautiful scenery found anywhere in North America.

59. Deer Hunting.

▲ A LEISURELY BREAK IN THE WOODS

Taking time out for a late morning rest, these five huntsmen have had a busy day. In addition to a fine doe, their bounty includes several foxes and a mixed bag of small game. These veteran woodsmen don't seem to be too worried about the antique weapons they are using, probably all of pre-Civil War vintage. Two of the old percussion muzzleloaders are double-barrel shotguns while three are rifles. Of special note, the muzzleloader leaning against the stump is equipped with a scope, probably an early "Wm. Malcolm" telescopic sight that measures nearly 3 feet in length. From a stereoview by the Kilburn Brothers, the scene was photographed in New England in the 1880s.

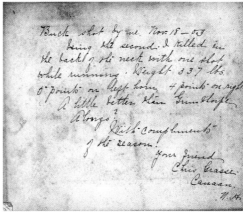

A NEW HAMPSHIRE HEAVYWEIGHT

This Kevin Costner look-alike proudly shows off a massive 9-point buck taken with what appears to be a Civil War vintage Springfield Model 1865 breechloading rifle, manufactured by U.S. Armory nearly 40 earlier in Springfield, Mass. The handwritten inscription on the back of the photo reads:

"Buck shot by me. Nov. 18 – 03. Being the second I killed
in the back of the neck with one shot while running.
Weight 337 lbs. 5 points on left horn, 4 points on right.
A little better than Grimthorpe Alonzo?
With compliments – of the season.
Your friend,
Chris Grasse
Canaan, N.H."

Note: The buck is quite huge, but doubtful that it weighed 337 pounds.

RARE WHITE DEER

Taxidermy was alive and well in 1892, as evidenced by this fully mounted piebald buck. Although it may be a far cry from the amazing works of art we commonly see in today's sophisticated taxidermy, the primitive mount is not bad considering it was done over 120 years ago. From a stereoview by B.W. Kilburn, titled "Albino or White Deer," dated 1892. The deer is a piebald instead of a true albino because of some patches of dark hair that show in the photo.

STEREOVIEW SERIES
MOOSE HUNT CAMP

⌃ UNLOADING GAME AT MOOSE HORN CAMP

It's December in the early 1900s in northern Maine's famed Aroostook County and it's been a very good day for the hunters at Moose Horn Camp. In this 1903 stereoview titled, "Big Bucks are Hard to Carry – Unloading Game at Moose Horn Camp," two men begin the demanding job of transporting the day's bounty from the horse-drawn sled to the camp meat pole.

⌃ A MAGNIFICENT SIGHT TO BEHOLD

The strenuous job of hanging seven heavy whitetails, including one very large buck, along with one bull moose has been completed and the majestic buck pole once again stands fully laden and strikingly picturesque with the spoils of the hunt. It is now time for the men to relax, admire their handiwork and reflect on the day's exciting adventures.

12258—Characteristic Camp Scene—Preparing for Supper and the Night

⌄ **PREPARING FOR SUPPER**

The men wash up and do their last minute outside chores before nightfall forces them to retire inside the cabin for a much anticipated meal. It will be another memorable evening of swapping stories and sharing that special brand of camaraderie found only in deer camp.

GAME LAWS OF MAINE—DEER.

CARIBOU.—It is unlawful to hunt the caribou before Oct. 15, 1905, six years' close time having been ordered by the legislature in 1899, when suit was brought against a firm having three caribou in possession each partner was held liable by the court.

MOOSE.—Hunting the moose cow or calf is prohibited at all times. The bull moose may be hunted between October 15th and December 1st. No person may kill or have in possession more than one bull moose.

DEER.—Common deer may be hunted between October 1 and December 15. No person may kill or have in possession more than two deer.

USE OF DOGS.—The use of dogs, snare traps and artificial lights is prohibited.

SUNDAY.—Sunday is a close day under the penalties imposed during the close season.

SPECIAL COUNTIES.—In certain counties the open season is limited to October, other counties are under a close time of six years.

PENALTIES.—Penalties are as high as $1,000 fine or four months imprisonment.—Public Laws of 1901.

PUBLIC GAME LAWS OF MAINE 1901

A DAY TO REMEMBER

Although this 105-year-old cabinet photo has seen its better days, it still contains enough life to tell a good story. Nov. 13, 1910, was a day this proud hunter would always remember. Unfortunately, that portion of the cardboard backing with his name and exact location in Maine has been broken off. Only the date remains. The huge buck was taken with a Winchester Model 1892 pistol grip, short-magazine rifle. The bullets around the hunter's waist could well be .25-20s, .32s or .38 WCFs, three popular rounds for that model. Compared to the man, this buck could weigh in excess of 250 pounds. The massive rack appears to be a main-frame 5-by-5 with split G-2s and several burr points. What a deer! What a day in the woods!

GREETINGS FROM NORTHERN MAINE

These two pipe-smoking gentleman hunters have struck pay dirt with two outstanding bucks taken in northern Maine on a snowy afternoon. Both carry the gun of choice in early 20th century Maine – a Winchester lever-action rifle. From a printed picture postcard circa 1915.

GREETINGS FROM NORTHERN MAINE.

ONE DAY'S BAG IN CARIBOU, MAINE

This photo postcard marked November 1909 depicts four hunters and their Winchester lever guns, along with their bag: four whitetails, including one bruiser buck, and four black bears. The handwritten note on the back of the postcard reads in part: "What do you think about this for one day's hunt?" Signed, "George." The card is postmarked Caribou, Maine (Aroostook County), 1909.

Once abundant throughout Maine, caribou were killed off by overhunting by the early 1900s. The last caribou from a native Maine herd was sighted on Mount Katahdin in 1908. During the past 70 to 80 years, all efforts to restore caribou to the state have failed due to poaching and predation.

TAKING THE BULL BY THE HORNS

Deep in the northern Maine forest, a fit young man totes a yearling buck out of the woods on his shoulders as his partner walks alongside. Photo circa 1920.

A fine young buck, a trusty Winchester rifle and a sharp knife with which to skin out his trophy – what more could a young man in the North Woods of Maine ask for? From a printed postcard titled "A Good Buck." The reverse side of this old postcard has the following rather confusing handwritten message:

"Mosquito, Me
Nov. 7, 1911

Dear Pa:
Guess this must be Linnie's picture
only the buck he got isn't quite as big.
Meet us Thurs. at Hollowell at 6:30 p.m.
                    With love from Vernon"

A Day's Outing in November, Bay Shore, L. I.

Made in Germany.   C. W. Race. Importer & Publisher. Bay Shore. L. I.. N. Y.

▲ MARKET HUNTING ON LONG ISLAND

Relaxed on the ground with his long-barrel muzzleloader, this content hunter is probably already counting the greenback dollars he will put in his pocket for such a large bag of venison that will no doubt end up in the markets of New York City. Market hunting on Long Island in the early 1900s became a serious problem for deer and the vast array of waterfowl found in the Great South Bay, and numbers of both were greatly depleted until modern game laws put an end to the excessive exploitation.

‹ PERFECT WEATHER
FOR A BIG BUCK

It's a cold, snowy day in Massachu-setts, but this proud hunter seems to be warm and cozy in his thick fur coat. He has plenty of reason to have that satis-fied look on his face. The stately buck tied across the front of his car has a large, multiple-point rack. The con-vertible car has a 1927 Massachusetts license plate. It is a pre-1920 model, possibly a 1917 or 1918 Packard, with a right-side steering wheel and head-lights mounted on the front fenders. This was his version of an early 20th century Jeep.

> **The American deer is fond of water, especially in the summer, and is often seen in shallow ponds feeding on wa-ter lilies. This they do most frequently at night which has led to a method of hunting them by boat. A light is placed at the bow, while the hunter is stationed in the shadow behind. The boat is then pushed quietly through the lily pads until a deer is seen or heard. Attracted by the light, the deer turns and faces it directly, thus making a perfect target.**

From a stereoview printed in the late 1890s.

◀ A "MOOSE" OF A WHITETAIL

This unusual nontypical "moose" of a whitetail was downed by Joseph Violette in November 1936. Joseph was a forest fire warden whose father was believed to be State Forest Commissioner Neil L. Violette, in the Allagash region of northern Maine. Reportedly, local hunters had been after this unique whitetail for several years because it possessed such an unusual and recognizable rack. The old warrior weighed 215 pounds, and was said to have had 55 distinct points on its highly palmated and bladed nontypical rack – if you could hang a ring on it, it was considered to be a point.

That number was no doubt an exaggeration, but at least 25 points can be easily counted in the photo, including several that have been broken on the left side and a 5- to 6-inch drop tine on the right. No matter how many points the rack possessed, this unusual whitetail must have been the trophy of a lifetime for the hunter who shot it. No one knows what eventually became of the trophy as it never appeared in any later record books compiled in Maine.

▲ AN EXTRAORDINARY SURPRISE IN THE MAINE WOODS

Mrs. Zina Witham and John E. Page of Augusta, Maine, were hunting together near Concord on Nov. 6, 1941, during the peak of the rut, when they came upon one of the most unusual scenes in the deer woods – two mature bucks hopelessly locked together in mortal combat. Judging from the half acre of torn-up ground around them, the two determined warriors had been going at it for several hours. After watching the spectacle for several minutes, the hunters approached the doomed 200-pound-plus bucks and quickly ended their ordeal with two well-placed bullets. Mr. Page was armed with a venerable Remington Model 8, while Mrs. Witham was using a Savage Model 99.

▲ HOW MUCH WILL YOU GIVE?

In the early 1900s, especially those years leading up to and through the tough Depression era of the 1930s, greenback dollars were hard to come by in northern Maine. If a man was lucky enough to shoot a good buck during the season, and if he was lucky enough to already have sufficient food to feed his family, it was a common practice to hang a buck by the road for any and all passersby to see. If someone wanted to buy the deer for the meat it would yield, they would stop by the house and negotiate a price, usually based on the estimated weight. A hefty 200-pound buck might go as high as $10 to $15 cash money. This form of barter became a well-known tradition in Maine before and during the Depression.

The young man pictured is holding a classic Winchester Model 1894 with a half-length magazine and a half-octagon barrel. Photo circa 1925.

SHARING A SPECIAL MEMORY

With their trusty rifles and smiles on their faces, these two hunting companions couldn't be more pleased with their good fortune in the wilds of Michigan. By their dress, these men are no doubt of European descent, possibly Swedes or Norwegians, but the Winchesters they carry are as American as apple pie. By the late 1800s, the virgin forests of northern Michigan had almost disappeared as evidenced by the apparent clear-cut terrain behind them. Even though the old-growth trees were gone forever, the new habitat created excellent browse for whitetails, grouse and other wildlife.

" The best way to kill whitetail is to still-hunt carefully through their haunts at dusk, when the deer leave the deep recesses in which their day-beds lie and come out to feed in the more open parts. For this kind of hunting, no dress is so good as the buckskin suit and moccasins. The moccasins enable one to tread softly and noiselessly, while the buckskin suit is of a most inconspicuous color, and makes less rustling than any other material when passing among projecting twigs. Care must be taken to always hunt upwind and to advance without any sudden motions, walking close in to the edge of the thickets and keeping a sharp lookout, as it is of the first importance to see the game before the game sees you. "

Theodore Roosevelt
Hunting Trips of a Ranchman, 1885

CHAPTER 4

THE RUGGED NORTH WOODS
CRADLE OF MIDWESTERN DEER HUNTING

Hardy explorers, hunters, settlers and pioneers steadily began to push westward from the eastern seaboard in the late 1600s and early 1700s, and the destinies of these early Americans were always closely mingled with whitetails. There was never a time when these courageous men and women did not depend on the continent's most popular big-game animal for food, because whitetails were found literally everywhere they traveled from the Georgia coast to the Northeast coast. As these hardy people moved westward across the Great Lakes region and the Ohio Valley, whitetails were always a primary source of food and a secondary source of clothing.

Hunting for whitetails did not originate in the Upper Midwest, but deer quickly became as important to the settlers as they had been in the Northeast and along the entire eastern seaboard during and after the establishment of the colonies. By the late 1800s, when European immigrants were settling the Upper Midwest around the Great Lakes, various ethnic groups began to find great pleasure in a pursuit that was purely an American original – going to deer camp and hunting whitetails each fall. And for good reason; like their cousins in the Northeast, the deer found in Michigan, Minnesota and Wisconsin were of the Northern Woodland subspecies. They carried the largest antlers and heaviest bodies of any deer on the continent.

Finns, Norwegians and Swedes soon found themselves looking forward to deer camp each fall. Somewhat less in numbers, the Polish, Romanians, Bulgarians, Italians and Germans quickly learned the basic skills needed for deer hunting and they couldn't wait to collect some venison for their families. These determined and innovative immigrants brought a wide variety of skills with them from the old country, but mostly they farmed. They fell in love with the native whitetails they encountered. By the mid-1800s, the Upper Midwest was rapidly becoming the cradle of deer hunting in America. Deer were hunted to such an extent in Wisconsin that by the late 1800s they were a rare sight in the southern portion of the state.

Getting into the vast North Woods of northern Michigan, Minnesota and Wisconsin was often a challenge to say the least. Lumber operations in the late 1800s remedied the problem somewhat by bringing rail access to many areas, and allowed hunters much easier travel north from high population areas. Once there, horse- or ox-drawn wagons and sleds were common methods of traveling those final few miles to deer camp. When all else failed, hiking in on foot from a rail line or the end of a road or wagon path was always a viable option.

The automobile changed everything in the early 1900s. Hunters could now go farther on their own and reach destinations never before deemed possible. In his classic book, *The Old Man and the Boy*, Robert Ruark immortalized his grandfather's old Model T, christened the "Tin Lizzie" in his hunting stories from the 1920s and '30s. Henry Ford's Model T and later the Model A revolutionized deer hunting. The Tin Lizzie did make travel easier, but there were still plenty of roadblocks along the way; flat tires, getting stuck in the mud and snow, overheated engines, and rough and washed-out wagon trails. But hunters persevered. Roads were built and improved, and the automobile became king.

By chance, one of the skills brought to the Midwest by European immigrants was the new-fangled art of photography. Simply because of the sheer number of professional photographers in the region, many thousands of deer hunting photos were taken depicting every facet of deer camp life in the great northern wilderness. As far as sheer numbers of hunting photos taken in the late 1800s and early 1900s, the Upper Midwest was one of the most photographed areas in the nation. Since friends, relatives and members of ethnic groups lived together, worked together and almost always hunted together, many of these old photos clearly delineate distinct nationalities like Norwegians and Swedes by the clothing and hats they wore.

Camping in the wilderness and hunting deer was certainly an enjoyable form of recreation, but these hard-working immigrant hunters seldom came home without a supply of meat for the winter. They were fast learners, they knew where to go and they knew how to find the deer they hunted. Thank goodness modern America has such an amazing photographic record to appreciate and treasure for all time.

◄ THE HUNTING WAS GOOD IN ONTONAGON

Armed to the teeth with mostly lever-action rifles, these nine men could resemble part of an infantry unit of Union soldiers preparing to do battle. Although some of their fathers and uncles likely fought in previous wars, the Winchesters and other modern rifles they are brandishing, and the sagging buck pole behind them clearly indicates that their quarry was of the four-legged variety. It is obvious here that some productive and memorable days were spent in the wilds of northern Michigan chasing after their favorite critters. The photo was taken near Ontonagon, Mich., around 1900. Located in the western edge of Michigan's Upper Peninsula, Ontonagon lies on the south shore of Lake Superior.

For well over 100 years, dedicated game wardens have risked life and limb to help stem the poaching of whitetails and other game and fish species across the U.S. and Canada. Since this uniformed gentleman is posed with a fine whitetail mount, we have to wonder, is he a turn-of-the century Michigan game warden? If so, was this deer killed illegally and was it confiscated? We'll never know the answer, but judging by his demeanor he definitely exudes an air of authority. Note the ankle-length fur coat he is wearing, which was very typical of the time period. Warm and plentiful, raccoon and buffalo coats were quite in style in the early 1900s and were a common sight, even in big cities like Chicago and New York.

Michigan became the first state to appoint a paid game warden in 1887. After years of uncontrolled market hunting for whitetails in the state during the late 1800s, a law was passed in 1895 that established a season and limit on the number of deer that could be harvested. The law also required the purchase of a license to hunt deer with a firearm. The cost was $0.50.

In 1914, after another sharp decline in deer numbers, the regulations were again changed to make antlered bucks the only legal deer that could be taken by hunters. By 1922, the state employed 180 full-time game wardens, and by the 1930s deer had rebounded to relatively large numbers.

Poaching dates back to medieval times when the privileged land barons and nobility in Europe tried to protect the game on their sprawling estates from the poor, hungry peasants who hunted mostly for food. During the 16th century, the crime of poaching a deer in England was punishable by death. Unfortunately, poaching is still a serious problem today in many parts of the world and modern-day poachers are motivated by greed and the monetary gain received from selling illegal animal parts. The battle against the poaching of whitetails is a dilemma that we've faced for several centuries now, and the huge interest in trophy antlers that has come about in recent decades has only worsened the problem.

Wanderings among the Wonders and Beauties of Wisconsin Scenery.

Photographed and Published by H. H. Bennett, Kilbourn City, Wis.

IN A CAMP OF DEER HUNTER'S.
Joe's good shot. No. 294.

▲ JOE'S GOOD SHOT

This vintage stereoview is titled, "In a Camp of Deer Hunters, Joe's good shot." Three of the hunters are armed with pre-Civil War muzzleloading long rifles, while the "renaissance" man on the left is armed with a state-of-the-art 1860 Henry repeater. Joe may be the man kneeling beside the buck. He is holding a finely crafted muzzleloader with inlays on the stock. A dog is curled up next to the hunter on the right. Published by H.H. Bennett, Kilbourn City, Wis. Circa late 1870s.

Photographed and Published by H. H. Bennett, Kilbourn City, Wis.

Wanderings among the Wonders and Beauties of Wisconsin Scenery.

IN A CAMP OF DEER HUNTERS
The way they leave them. No. 293.

▲ IN A CAMP OF DEER HUNTERS – THE WAY THEY LEAVE THEM

Despite the fact that most early 20th century deer hunters judged their success by the meat they brought home rather than the size of a buck's headgear, no true hunter would ever pass up a chance to hang a splendid buck like this on the buck pole for all to see. Photographed and published by well-known photographer H.H. Bennett in the Wisconsin Dells area, circa 1900.

⌃ **DOUBLING UP ON A WISCONSIN "TWO-FER"**

This happy Wisconsin farm boy has good reason to be smiling – two fine bucks that will no doubt keep his family in venison through the upcoming winter. Judging by his work clothes – bib overalls and lightweight shirt, and the fact that there is no snow on the ground, the weather must have been fairly mild. Did both bucks fall to his trusty Winchester lever action or did another hunter, perhaps a kid brother not pictured, put one of these bucks on the ground?

The first bag limits in Wisconsin were set in 1897; allowing two deer per season with the cost of a resident license being $1. The limit was lowered to one deer per season in 1909 when deer became scarce due to the effects of market hunting. Since this old cabinet photo was taken in the very early 1900s, it's entirely possible that the young man could have legally taken both bucks. If so, he no doubt enjoyed sharing some exciting tales with his grandchildren in later years about his most memorable day ever in the Wisconsin woods.

⌃ **SAGGING BUCK POLE**

Three serious hunters pose with the fruits of their labor in northern Wisconsin as a sagging buck pole holds five large-bodied white-tails and one snowshoe hare. From a printed lithographic postcard made by E.C. Kropp, Milwaukee, Wis. Circa 1908.

This vintage postcard records a very successful hunting scene near the north-central Minnesota town of Akeley, in 1909.

◄ **SEVEN DEER IN SEVEN DAYS FOR SEVEN HUNTERS**

One glorious week of hunting near Park Falls, Wis., produced seven hefty bucks for these seven proud hunters in November 1924. The two hunters standing at each end are brandishing long-barrel Winchesters. The photo was taken by G. Toburen, of Wausau, Wis., a well-known studio photographer in the early 1900s.

⌃ STARS AND STRIPES FOREVER – EVEN IN DEER CAMP

Written on the back of this photo postcard dated November 1910 are the words: "John and hunting party." We don't know which of these rugged hunters might be John, but the entire group, including two women, no doubt enjoyed a few memorable days camping and chasing big-bodied whitetails in the North Country of Wisconsin or Minnesota. The results speak for themselves. The camp is definitely an ethnic group of European descent. Note the man holding the small American Flag.

⌃ THE BIG MINNESOTA CHILL

It's a cold and icy day in northern Minnesota as evidenced by the two large does and buck that are frozen solid, along with the black bear that is leaning over the fence and posing nicely for the photo. The three sportsmen are grinning and baring it, as if to say, "Let's get this over with so we can go inside and warm up." This photo was yet another gem snapped by gifted Minnesota photographer W.T. Oxley, circa early 1920s. The hunter on the left is holding an 1899 .30-40 Krag rifle while the man in the middle appears to be holding a Remington pump-action rifle. Photo courtesy of Rich Oxley.

⋏ AN IMPRESSIVE PILE OF BONE

This mountain of venison and enormous antlers, including a mammoth 20-something-point nontypical giant that has several broken tines in the center of the heap, is being prepared to ship out by rail courtesy of the Grand Rapids and Indiana Railway. The lucky hunters who bagged these deer in northern Michigan were on their way back to the big cities in the southern part of the state.

The historic railroad got its humble beginnings in the late 1860s, but it was not until the mid-1870s that it began to prosper, hauling lumber out of the virgin forests of northern Michigan. Once the forests were depleted, the railroad concentrated on its passenger business in the late 1800s, helping to open up what had once been endless wilderness to settlement. By around 1915, when this photo was taken in Pellston, Mich., the railroad had long passed its heyday. We can't be sure if the smiling young men in the photo are railroad workers or several of the proud hunters, but judging from the size of the racks on these deer, someone had a mighty good week of hunting the woods of northern Michigan!

W.T. OXLEY

Walter Theodore "W.T." Oxley (1872-1955) was a well-known and gifted Minnesota photographer who later operated a studio with his son Lloyd from around 1910 to 1930. He spent much of his prime in the early 1900s traveling from town to town making photo postcards. During his long, distinguished career, he photographed such luminaries as the Wright Brothers, Theodore Roosevelt and Buffalo Bill Cody. Being an avid whitetail hunter, he traveled to northern Minnesota each season with friends to hunt North America's largest-bodied deer.

Baudette is located in north-central Minnesota only a stone's throw from the border with Ontario. W.T. and his hunting companions often traveled in and out of the backcountry in the area on a wooden sled pulled by oxen. The hunters would set up camp and attempt to live off the land for up to two weeks. Although deer hunting was the primary objective, W.T. seldom separated himself from his large-format camera. Now, 100 years later, the legacy he left behind of those golden days can be measured by the incredible photographic record that has been preserved by his grandson, Richard Oxley. Most of W.T.'s photos were made on large glass negatives, giving them an enduring sharpness. More importantly, he had an eye for composition that few photographers ever attain. He was an artist with a camera.

A GOOD DOG, A GOOD RIFLE AND A GRAND WAY OF LIFE IN GOD'S COUNTRY

This pipe-smoking North Woods trapper is obviously in his element. With his homemade buckskin jacket and his game-getting Model 1898 Krag-Jorgensen that has no doubt put plenty of venison and moose meat on the table, one quick glance around his remote cabin makes it clear that he knows his way around the woods. Bear skins, deer skins, beaver pelts, an otter or two, a moose antler and at least one whitetail rack – these are the prizes of his efforts.

With the same trusty Krag-Jorgensen and same faithful dog by his side, our North Woods trapper has just assured himself of plenty of moose meat for the winter. During his annual excursions to the area, photographer W.T. Oxley often stopped by the remote cabin of this trapper and took photos. The man's name is lost to the ages, but he lived off the land on a year-round basis and prospered in the northern wilderness only a few miles from the Canadian border. Photos by W.T. Oxley, courtesy of grandson Richard Oxley.

WINCHESTERS WIN THE DAY

These four Winchester-toting hunters know how to fill up a buck pole. The man on the left holds a Winchester Model 1907 semiautomatic, while his three partners in crime are all armed with Winchester lever-action rifles. The photo was taken near Baudette, Minn., around 1920 by W.T. Oxley. Photo courtesy of Richard Oxley.

WHAT MORE COULD A HUNTER ASK FOR?

This proud Michigan woodsman, dressed warmly in wool, has certainly earned bragging rights on the day's bag. Posed with a fine Maxwell touring car that obviously got him to and from his secret hunting grounds, and a trusty Marlin lever-action rifle that once again has proven its worth as more than a match for a hefty Michigan bruin and a fine whitetail buck, this young man has had an unforgettable day. At first glance, it appears as though the hunter is holding a cigarette in his right hand. However, closer inspection reveals a spent high-powered cartridge, possibly a .30-30.

A predecessor of the ever-popular Chrysler brand, the 1924 "Good Maxwell" touring car sold for between $885 and $1,485. Gasoline was $0.25 per gallon, and the average annual income in America was about $2,200. Maxwell Motor Company was bought out by Walter Chrysler in 1923. Today, the rifle this lucky hunter is holding could easily be worth more than the original cost of his car. Photo circa 1924.

GREETINGS FROM SCOTTVILLE, MICHIGAN

As several hunters stand in the background admiring the overloaded buck pole, this 1940 photo postcard from central Michigan depicts seven fine bucks – including one outstanding 10-pointer – and an exceptional Michigan bruin. Photo postcard by L. L. Cook Co., 1940.

A MINNESOTA WALLHANGER

These two Minnesota hunters have much to celebrate. It's not often you come home with a gnarly 8-pointer like this. No doubt this big boy is going on the wall. The hunter on the right is holding a Winchester carbine. While the lever gun on the left also appears to be a Winchester at first glance, further scrutiny reveals that it is in fact a beautiful Savage Model 99. The car is a 1941 Dodge. Photo circa early 1940s.

⌃ PROUD TO BE AMERICAN DEER HUNTERS

The wide front fenders of this 1937 Nash Lafayette make the perfect spots for transporting these two Wisconsin bucks home from deer camp. These happy deerslayers have just pulled up in the driveway and are in the process of unloading the smallest of the two so that they can process the meat. Old Glory flies proudly on the front bumper. The license tag indicates the year is 1940. Little could these two hunters imagine that America would be engaged in a terrible world war the following year.

⌃ Six bucks on the buck pole, taken near Houghton Lake, Prudenville, Mich., 1940.

◄ HOLDING DOWN THE FORT IN MICHIGAN

This stoic Michigan hunter, who is perhaps too old to be fighting in the war, has to be walking on clouds after the day he and his deer hunting partner have had.

Both bucks have bragging-size racks. The buck on the right has a beautiful, long-tined, 8-point rack while the buck our gentleman hunter is standing beside is a smaller but much heavier 8-pointer with several stickers and odd points. The automobile is a 1940 Chrysler. Photo taken in 1942.

⋀ ANOTHER FINE TROPHY FOR THE DOC

Avid whitetail hunter Dr. Noland Eidsmore of Rice Lake poses with an outstanding Wisconsin trophy whitetail during the 1947 season. Three deer came out of the heavy timber to his left and he put his sights on the largest. He is holding two rifles; one appears to be a Winchester lever action, the other a Remington Model 14 pump. Dr. Eidsmore was also a dedicated trout fisherman. He wrote a number of hunting and fishing articles for *Midwest Outdoors* in the 1940s and '50s. Photo by E. A. Thomas.

OF LEGENDS AND OBSESSIONS

Two tremendous bucks have just arrived in a snowy camp in the back of a wagon – one very wide, the other carrying a very heavy frame. These are no ordinary whitetails. Both deer are enormous. In today's world, this pair would be considered the bucks of many lifetimes, the kinds of animals that grow into local legends and become obsessions. A hunter lucky enough to shoot one of these bucks would no doubt put it in his trophy room and cherish it for years to come. Photo circa early 1900s.

" The whitetail is the only one of our deer that can live contentedly and unsuspectedly in a hundred acres of thicket. It is the only one that, hearing a hostile footfall, will sneak around to find the cause, study its trail, and then glide, cat-like, through the brush to a farther haven, without even trying to see the foe who thus gets no chance for a shot. It is the least migratory, the least polygamous, the least roving, as well as the swiftest, keenest, shyest, wisest, most prolific, and most successful of our deer. It is the only one that has added to its range; that in the North and West has actually accompanied the settler into the woods; that has followed afar into newly opened parts of New England and Canada; that has fitted its map to man's, and that can hold its own on the frontier.

The whitetail is the American deer of the past and the American deer of the future. "

Ernest Thompson Seton
The Nature Library – Animals, 1926

CHAPTER 5

A PASSEL OF BONE & BUCKSKIN

There were numerous reasons to go to the deer woods in the fall; thousands of starlit hunting destinations in remote locations where big bucks reportedly hid behind every tree. Tens of thousands of bright-eyed hunters flocked to the autumn woods to seek adventure, a few memorable days in the wilderness and the camaraderie of deer camp.

They came from all walks of life. They were butchers and bankers, mill and factory workers, hard-working farmers, carpenters, doctors, Civil War veterans, and men who had been at San Juan Hill with Theodore Roosevelt. They were city boys and country boys. They were young boys and old men, grandfathers, sons, uncles and cousins. They were men whose families had immigrated to America. The men and women of those determined families had stubbornly rolled up their sleeves and helped build a fledgling country from the ground up. They were of all nationalities and they traveled to deer camp together — Swedes, Norwegians, Finns, Italians, Poles, Hungarians, Germans, Russians, English and French.

They were willing to leave their comfortable homes and knowingly withstand considerable hardships — bitter cold, snow and ice, everything the harsh winter climate could throw at them. They purposely traveled to unforgiving landscapes that still belonged to Mother Nature in

every sense of the word. In fact, they welcomed Nature's many challenges with open arms and a sense of arrogance because it was part of the experience. There was a job to be done. The quest for meat and the sheer thrill of the hunt were two of the driving motivations. Big antlers were always a bonus, but venison was the ultimate and most cherished prize. Hunters judged their successes by the number of deer hanging on the camp meat pole.

To reach camp, they trekked long miles on foot, sometimes using snowshoes when the snow drifts were deep. Others arrived by horseback, in buggies and in horse- or ox-drawn wagons and sleds. Still others used the railroad, often flagging down trains, heading north and setting out in remote areas. Later, when Henry Ford's revolutionary "tin lizzy" began to replace the horse and wagon, the automobile reached new vistas by taking hunters farther from home than they ever dreamed possible — and in much less time. Some adventurous souls even used motorcycles with names like Indian and Harley Davidson.

On a typical day in the woods they traveled light, taking with them only the bare necessities — warm clothes, usually wool, waterproof boots if available, gloves, a good knife, matches, a few extra bullets, a length of rope with which to drag their deer, and often a compass. No frills except for the most important item of all — a rifle. Seasoned hunters all shared one thing in common – to the man, they always felt a special kinship with their rifles.

A man's rifle was the one piece of equipment that was almost part of him. It was part of a deer hunter's psyche; always carried with pride, loved, cherished and well taken care of.

They assembled once a year in their rustic hideouts in the woods. Often they had to repair leaky roofs, rid the cabin of rats that had declared ownership in their absence, and make other temporary "quick fix" repairs so that their cramped abodes would be livable for a few days or a few weeks. They brought with them everything needed to survive – food, sometimes hard drink, axes, saws and other vital camp necessities.

They shared a glorious week of laughing, telling jokes and tall tales, playing pranks, dealing cards at night and sometimes drinking more than they should. Early each morning, long before daylight, they awakened, drank hot coffee and ate a hardy breakfast, dressed as warmly as possible, and trudged out across the newly fallen snow to secret locations where they hoped that fate would shower them with the blessing of a fine buck.

They cut wood for the fire, oiled their rifles, hunted small game for the pot and relished in other camp chores. They hung their bounty on a sagging meat pole, and proudly beamed and reflected at their amazing accomplishments as deer hunters. When it was all over, they reluctantly packed their gear and headed back to civilization. No one on the home front could ever comprehend the true significance of being in deer camp or just how important the experience was in the lives of these unconventional adventurers.

Only another hunter could understand the true essence of what it meant to caress a beloved rifle, fight off the cold on a frigid, snowy morning, observe a graceful whitetail buck bounding through the woods, and get lost in one's thoughts while staring into the flames and embers of a life-giving fire each night.

It was a brotherhood that not everyone was suited to be a part of, a well-kept secret that only a chosen few were able to participate in and savor, namely because it took a certain amount of grit and stubborn determination. But, those members of this elite club walked a little taller, stood a little straighter and lived their lives with a greater degree of self confidence and self sufficiency than most outsiders might ever be able to understand; for those remarkable men were of a different breed. They had earned the right to call themselves American whitetail hunters.

Killed near Hill City, S. Dak.

◀ **BLACK HILLS GOLD – SOUTH DAKOTA'S FINEST**

This bag of two outstanding bucks, one spike and two does was taken near Hill City, S.D., in 1909. The young man on the left has a fancy sporting Winchester lever action with a half magazine and pistol grip, while his two partners on the right are holding more standard-style Winchester lever actions. Hill City is just southwest of Rapid City in the Black Hills. A mere 20 years before this photo was taken, much of this country was still controlled by the mighty Sioux Nation.

A TOLERABLE PASSEL OF BONE AND BUCKSKIN

Most whitetail hunters may hunt for a lifetime and never witness anything close to this incredible collection of massive bucks, at least not in one place. Stacked in this Wells Fargo Express wagon like so much cordwood, this extraordinary load of bone and buckskin is no doubt headed to the train depot where it will be shipped to a large city like St. Paul or Chicago. Local residents will soon be purchasing choice cuts in butcher shops or dining on fine morsels of venison in expensive restaurants. The Wells Fargo agent seems to understand how special the moment is, as does the boy in the front.

This amazing collection of "horns" was almost certainly procured by market hunters, probably in northern Wisconsin or northern Minnesota, shortly before the turn of the century when no bag limits and no seasons prevailed. Photo circa 1890.

A REAL ATTENTION-GETTER

It's anybody's guess as to whether or not the Remington Model 8 held by the man on the left or the Winchester Model 1895 held by the man clutching a tine on the right did the deed, but one of these fortunate hunters has earned bragging rights on this magnificent 11-pointer. The man on the far right also cradles a '95 Winchester topped with a period MSA Company tang sight. These rugged hunters could be Maine potato farmers, backwoodsmen from Kentucky or West Virginia, or anywhere in between. One thing is clear – they have plenty to celebrate. Bucks like this are few and far between. Photo circa 1910.

On the left border: *Keystone View Company. Manufacturers and Publishers*

On the right border: *Meadville, Pa., St. Louis, Mo. Copyright 1901, by B. L. Singley*

11632—Contemplating the Prize.

▲ CONTEMPLATING THE PRIZE

Two hunters admire a fine buck after a fresh snow in the Northeast. The man kneeling has a Winchester repeater across his lap; the man standing has a Savage Model 99 leaning against the tree. From a stereoview titled, "Contemplating the Prize," by Keystone View Company, Meadville, Pa., and St. Louis, Mo., dated 1901.

◄ HOME FROM THE HILL

This beaming sportsman has arrived home with a stockpile of meat for the coming months – two prime young whitetail bucks, a black bear and several snowshoe hares. The vehicle looks like a delivery truck with a commercial license plate that has been decked out for hunting, complete with two extra tires for any trouble in the backcountry. The license plate has a 1914 date but the state is not visible. Without a doubt, the trusty lever-action Winchester – a Model 1892 or 1894 – our hero is holding has once again proven its worth.

⌃ A MEMORABLE FAMILY OUTING

The first thing your eyes feast upon in this vintage photo are the huge antlers on the 10-pointer. Then you notice that the lady of the house has taken possession of this incredible animal by placing her hand on one antler. Did she outdo everyone else on the hunt? Is that her husband on her right, her two sons on her left and perhaps "Uncle Bob" with the glass flask in his belt?

It's likely these are all members of the same family and they seem to take the business of deer hunting very seriously. They are extremely well armed with the latest in high-tech firearms. On the left, Uncle Bob is holding a sure-shooting Winchester Model 1907 semiautomatic chambered in the .351 Self-Loading round. Next to him, the pistol-toting father of the clan is clutching an ever-dependable Remington Model 8. The matriarch of the family is holding a handsome Marlin 1893 lever action, while the boy on her left has an identical rifle. The second son appears to be holding the same rifle as Uncle Bob, a Winchester Model 1907 semiautomatic. Photo circa 1910-1915.

⌃ PINCH ME... I MUST BE DREAMING

This proud hunter's body language says it all. With pure admiration and awe in his face, the picture communicates an endless narrative that has been acted out a million times around a million different campfires across America over the past 150 years. The rifle is an iconic Remington Model 8. The photo is from the 1920s, and the location could be almost anywhere in the North Country.

⊲ A PROUD MOMENT

With three bucks hanging, two of which own impressive racks, these hunters should feel a sense of deep satisfaction with their achievement. The man on the left is leaning on his trusty Winchester Model 1895, while the man in the middle has a bolt-action sporting rifle, a popular Savage Model 20. The other two rifles appear to be Winchester carbines. The old cabinet photo portrait was captured in northwestern Pennsylvania by photographer E.F. Sell, of Union City. Circa early 1920s.

⊳ WHAT A SET OF HORNS!

Do you think this lucky hunter might have gotten a slight case of buck fever when this moose of a whitetail stepped into his sights? We'll never know what his precise reaction was, but he obviously exercised enough control to make the shot count. Showing off his Winchester Model 94 as well as his magnificent trophy, he seems totally calm and collected. The awesome 10-pointer is lashed across the front of a 1928 Auburn touring car. Auburn cars were popular in the 1920s, but the Great Depression of the 1930s spelled doom for the company.

With a mountainous background, it is hard to say just where this slayer of big bucks might have crossed paths with such an massive deer, but Pennsylvania or New York is a reasonable guess. Photo circa late 1920s.

⊲ ADMIRING A REAL BEAUTY

This impressive old monarch of the woods probably turned more than a few heads as he made the long trip home on the front fender of the 1931 or '32 Buick. Now it's time for this proud deerslayer to reflect a moment, pay his respects and admire his handiwork. The rack seems to have had an injury to its left antler, resulting in a short drop tine. The delighted hunter is holding a popular Remington Model 14 with a tang sight. Photo circa early 1930s.

More American
Reserve Power

*Painted for Remington UMC
by F. X. Leyendecker*

BOTH to the man himself and to all about him, the strength that comes from the hills is invaluable today.

No poison-pollen of Old World imperialism gone to seed can contaminate— nor any attempt of crowd-sickened collectivism undermine—the priceless individualism of the American who truly keeps his feet on the earth.

Are you one of America's five million hunters, planning a trip for big game—and reserve power?

Our Service Department will be glad to help you complete arrangements—tell what to take, if you wish—report on hunting districts—give addresses and rates of best hunting camps and guides.

Or ask your local dealer, the alert Remington UMC merchant—one of more than 82,700 in this country—whose store is your community Sportsmen's Headquarters.

Guides, Outfitters, Camp Proprietors—Write for registration blank for Remington UMC free service.

THE REMINGTON ARMS UNION METALLIC CARTRIDGE CO., *Inc.*
Largest Manufacturers of Firearms and Ammunition in the World
WOOLWORTH BUILDING   NEW YORK

➤ **A RUTTING BEAST**

Do you suppose this gnarly ol' mossback met his demise like so many hapless bucks often do – by being caught out in the open while chasing after a seemingly harmless doe? How else would such a vigilant denizen of the forest find himself in front of a hunter's rifle? One thing is certain. This is one happy young man. Photo circa 1930s.

◄ **A BRUTE**

This hunter has plenty of reason to be smiling. He has just taken a true monster weighing well over 250 pounds with his sporterized Krag-Jorgensen rifle. Note the strutting domestic turkey to the right of the wide spreading 10-point rack. It's a good thing our hero is hunting big bucks instead of turkeys.

◄ **A GOOD DAY'S SPORT**

This exhilarated hunting couple may be floating on clouds instead of water after the day they've enjoyed beating the bushes in the Muskoka Lakes region of Ontario, Canada, which is about 100 miles north of Toronto. The gorgeous 11-point trophy buck with a broken tine on the right side was well worth any and all effort expended. We'll never know if the man or his friend shot this magnificent animal, but the lady certainly knows how to handle a canoe. Photo circa late 1920s to early 1930s.

THREE GENERATIONS OF HUNTERS

Are we in Kansas yet? It's never easy for hard-working farmers to take off and play hooky from the rigors of the farm, but this happy crew apparently did just that. Look at the results, they certainly have found the Land of Oz. Grandpa got Old Brutus, Dad came home with a fine 8-pointer, and Junior may be too young to hunt, but proudly gets to take charge of the arsenal – an octagon-barrel Winchester lever-action rifle and a short-barrel Winchester carbine.

The deer will soon be hung in the barn for skinning and butchering and the guns will have to be cleaned and oiled. The telephone pole in the background indicates this farm family has electricity, and the 1930s-era Model A Ford suggests the photo was taken in the Midwest farm belt in the late 1930s.

IF A TROPHY DEER COULD TALK...

Modern whitetail hunting has seen its share of setup photos designed to provoke a laugh or two, but vintage photos like this one are rare indeed. This reversed role photo of the hunter on the fender was taken somewhere up in the snowy North Country in the late 1930s or early '40s. The automobile is a 1935 Plymouth that has weathered more than a few memorable seasons in deer camp. Typical of the period is the hunter's plaid coat. The rifle on the hood of the car is the ever-popular Remington Model 8. If that big buck could talk, he would probably have a humdinger of a story to tell!

A FINE BUCK, A FINE DAY IN QUEBEC

This proud hunter stands next to his hefty 10-pointer and a bear on the porch beside it. The photo postcard reads: "A Fine Buck, Matapedia, P.Q., Quebec, Canada." Matapedia is located in eastern Quebec near the New Brunswick border. The area has long been known for its superb hunting, fishing and outdoor recreation. The rifle is a reliable pump action, possibly a Remington Model 25. Photo circa 1935.

END OF THE HUNT

These hunters must be delighted with the results of their hunt. After a successful outing in central Ontario, they are taking a lunch break as they prepare for the trip home. Their duffels and other gear are packed and ready to be loaded aboard the long boats that will take them across the lake. Several outstanding bucks lay among the rocks, including one behemoth with a wide-spreading rack and long tines that may well be of record-book caliber. Photo circa mid-1930s.

> ◄ **BASEBALL, CHEVROLETS,**
> **APPLE PIE AND BIG BUCKS**

Although he doesn't appear dressed for the occasion, this shotgun-wielding hunter has done a good day's work as he proudly chews on his stogie and shows off a heavily framed old monarch that won't be chasing does any longer. Behind him sits his 1941 Chevrolet Deluxe. The shotgun is a 1930s-vintage Browning Auto-5 12 gauge, popular for waterfowl and upland bird hunting in the mid-20th century, and also used by a fair number of deer hunters, particularly when hunting with hounds in the Deep South.

> ➤ **MR. GERMAIN'S**
> **CHRISTMAS BOUNTY**

From a photo postcard dated Dec. 29, 1948, and post-marked Bellingham, Wash., this outstanding buck with split brow tines is indeed an answer to a Christmas prayer. Mr. Germain, the proud hunter, stands next to his prize wearing a checkered wool shirt and posing with a vintage military rifle. The barrel tip looks suspiciously like that of a Springfield Model 1903 .30-06. Bellingham is located near the coast in western Washington, but the buck was probably taken in the eastern part of the state where white-tails were more common in the late 1940s.

△ BLUE GRASS DREAM BUCK

Although this yet-to-be-field-dressed Kentucky 11-pointer barely fits into the trunk of the 1950s automobile, the two smiling hunters don't seem to mind. They're floating on clouds. The year on the license plate appears to be 1956. Could these two men have served their country with distinction during World War II a just over decade earlier? If so, they certainly have earned the right to spend a few memorable days in the whitetail woods pursuing America's most challenging big-game animal.

➤ THE REDCOATS ARE COMING AND THEY'RE TAKING NO PRISONERS

This wool-coated gentleman hunter wearing rubber boots and donning a license on his back looks over the brute of a trophy buck that obviously fell to one of the two rifles leaning against the tree earlier that day: one is a slick lever-action Savage 99 with a scope, and the other is a bolt-action sporter, possibly a Winchester Model 54. Since the hunter is wearing a permit on his back, he may well be in Wisconsin, New York or Pennsylvania. The photo was taken after World War II, in the late 1940s or early 1950s.

Scenes from a typical 1920s-era hunting club.

> **Oh, a good buck track just sets me to quivering!**

Larry Benoit
How to Bag the Biggest Buck of Your Life, 1974

CHAPTER 6

GLORIOUS, WONDERFUL DEER CAMP

Ah, deer camp. You can almost smell the winter woods, feel the chill of the northern wind, hear the crunch of the new-fallen snow, and savor the aroma of steaks and potatoes cooking over an open flame. The welcome scent of evergreens and woodsmoke conjures up memories of large-bodied bucks and frosty November mornings. A week in deer camp with good company is about as close to heaven as a man can get.

Most hunters of yesteryear were not picky about their deep-woods accommodations. Deer-camp quarters were expected to be rustic and primitive – and often they were just that. At worst, the most basic requirement that hunters hoped to realize was a place to stay dry and warm at night. At best, lavish cabins built by more affluent individuals or clubs offered nearly all the comforts of home. For those seasoned groups of hunters who had been at it awhile, most cabins offered a fireplace for warmth, or a wood-burning stove for cooking and heat, a sturdy table for eating and playing cards, and some creaky bunk beds. Uncomfortable as they usually were, they offered the promise of a few hours of rest for weary bones and muscles after a long day in the elements.

Cabins, shacks and primitive shelters came in all sizes and shapes. They were as varied and diverse as the hunters who used them. In cold weather, wilderness hunters constantly on the move often made temporary shelters out of pine boughs and saplings that were suitable for a night or two of camping. Those shelters might have been large enough to sleep three or four men. Of course, if the weather permitted, one could sleep out under the stars next to the fire.

Those individuals not fortunate enough to have a cabin often had to improvise with tents. For trips lasting a week or longer, large wall tents were usually furnished with some sort of stove for cooking and staying warm in subfreezing temperatures. Here you could store your food, bedding and gear and keep things relatively dry.

Some cabins or shacks, occupied only once a year during deer season, were ofttimes in a dilapidated state of repair after bears, porcupines and other creatures of the wild had gotten inside and ransacked the place during the off-season. Some wilderness cabins were small and cramped one-room affairs. Others were more spacious with a main living area and a large bunk room holding beds or cots.

No matter what size or shape they happened to come in, and no matter what state of repair they were found to be in at the beginning of the new season, these much-loved structures became home-sweet-home for a few days or weeks. Despite the frustrations of leaking roofs, snowflakes and raindrops blowing in between the cracks, no indoor facilities, no electricity and no running water, these rustic cabins in the wilderness were a pure piece of outdoor paradise.

TENTING IN THE WILDERNESS

◄ BEARS IN THE MIX

Seeing a couple of big bruins hanging alongside several nice bucks on a meat pole always grabs the heart of any true hunter, and it definitely adds a special dimension to deer camp. This picture could be almost anywhere, but with the open rolling hills, it is quite reminiscent of upstate New York, southern Pennsylvania or West Virginia. The split rail fence in the distance indicates that these hardy outdoorsmen have set up their camp on someone's sprawling farm. All of the men appear to be holding lever-action rifles – Winchesters and Marlins. Photo circa 1910.

► I WONDER WHAT THE POOR FOLKS ARE DOING TODAY?

A picturesque setting on the water, a smattering of snow on the ground, a contented hound and a good canoe to get you over to that dead water where Old Goliath has been hiding; what more could a dedicated group of hunters ask for? The rifles have spoken again and this tranquil deer camp near Ashland, Wis., far up on the southern edge of Lake Superior, is buzzing with activity. The two men to the right of the tent are surely toasting to the camp's good fortune. This printed postcard dates around 1910 to 1920.

A SEASON LIKE NO OTHER

Several bruiser bucks can be seen among the deer hanging in this cozy deer camp, all brought down with quintessentially American lever-action rifles. The hardy Scandinavian group and their camp existed in northern Minnesota or Wisconsin. Photo circa 1910.

DEEP WOODS DEERSLAYERS

Based on the way they are grinning, it's an even bet that one of these two pipe-smoking deerslayers is responsible for the massive 10-pointer hanging up in this deep-woods camp. No location is given, but it's a cinch there will be much celebrating going on tonight! Photo circa 1930s.

PENNSYLVANIA DEER CAMP, 1923

Looks like these men have done themselves proud; the happy crew has put plenty of venison on the buck pole. No, this isn't the Penn State football team and their coaches, though several of these young men do look athletic enough to play college football. A few of these vibrant All-American boys may well have fought in World War I just a few years earlier. Now they are all looking for a few days of special camaraderie and serenity that can only be found in deer camp.

◄ **MODERN ROBIN HOODS**

During the historic second annual bow hunt held at Rock Creek Game Refuge in the North Georgia Mountains in early November 1941, these three veteran bowmen have just finished their early morning breakfast outside comfortable, wooden-floor wall tents and are preparing to head to the woods. The media dubbed this as "the only deer hunt organized especially for archers in the United States." From left to right are Phil Cozad of Columbus, Ohio; Dick Barbour of Atlanta, Ga.; and Lou Ribble of Richmond, Va. All three hunters attended the first historic hunt the year before in 1940. Much to their chagrin, not a single deer was taken during that inaugural hunt. They were determined to change the situation in 1941.

▶ **WOODCUTTING CHORES**

The woodcutting chores in deer camp are never ending. It takes a lot of wood to keep the wood stove fired up, especially at night when that cold North wind begins to howl through the forest. Photo dated December 1919.

THE DEER SHACK

▽ A COZY DEER CAMP

After a long day's tramp chasing gnarly whitetails, these four seasoned long-rifle hunters have erected a fine weatherproof shelter out of evergreen saplings and boughs. Now they are enjoying a well-earned respite as they warm themselves by the fire, wait for supper to cook in the large pot, and admire the considerable pile of venison and bone stacked in front – including one whopper buck. Titled "Deer Hunter's camp in the Northwest," this vintage stereoview was made in the northwestern portion of the Adirondacks of New York around 1880.

➤ A FEAST FOR THE EYES

It's a cold and snowy day somewhere in the North Country as this hunting family admires the fruits of their labor in front of a very stout cabin. The patriarch of the family holds two fine rifles – a Winchester and a Marlin. His wife and son each hold a rifle as well. This family has much to be proud of. Photo circa 1900.

▼ NORTH POLE EXPRESS

With icicles dangling from the roof, this wonderful photo gives us a perfect window into what camp life was like in the North Country after a heavy snow 100 years ago. Cabin fever and a break in the weather have brought this group of veteran deerslayers out into the bitter cold to show off their bounty and forever capture the moment on film. Taken in the Midwest, everything is covered in fresh snow, including several of the bucks. You can't knock success, and these hardy souls have seen plenty of that. Photo circa early 1900s.

▼ SNOWBOUND

Woodsmoke drifting out of the chimney of this snowbound cabin in the middle of nowhere gives the sense of warmth and security. It is large enough to accommodate a sizable group of hunters. Judging by all of the snow-covered clutter in the yard, the place apparently sees a lot of use. It is possible that this cabin has been wired for electricity as several wires lead into the right side of the shack. Photo circa 1925.

▲ A DIAMOND IN THE ROUGH

This crude log cabin in the North Country is not the most sophisticated or appealing structure in the world, but at least it affords a roof overhead and a place to stay warm and dry when the weather turns raw. The large pile of cabin-size logs behind the two hunters hint that a new structure is in the works. Photo circa 1910.

RUSTIC ON THE OUTSIDE AND WARM INSIDE

Judging by the size of several very impressive bucks, including one "moose" of a whitetail with a nontypical rack, Kamp Kounter must be located in the wilds of northern Minnesota or Wisconsin. Photo circa 1920.

MICHIGAN HUNTING SCENE

Standing beside their tar-papered cabin christened "The Smear," deep in the woods near Newberry, Mich., these two happy hunters have done well. Newberry is in the Upper Peninsula, and in more recent times has been designated the "moose capital" of Michigan. Dated Nov. 5, 1909, (the year the Lincoln penny was released in commemoration of Abe Lincoln's 100th birthday) the somewhat confusing printed postcard bears the inscription: "Newberry, No/5/09 - Bill - First night on the Shotgun." The Shotgun could be a nearby river or lake in the area, but who knows where the name "The Smear" originated or what it stands for? Both rifles are lever-action guns and their accuracy during the hunt is apparent.

AT HOME IN REMINGTON CAMP

The name "Remington Camp," on the side of this deer shack may be an appropriate designation as two of the hunters standing in the midst of several hanging deer are holding Remington pump-action rifles – Model 14s or Model 25s. Of course, the man on the right with his hand on the small buck obviously is going against the grain with his lever action. Judging by the 1925 or 1926 Studebaker, the photo was taken in the mid- to late 1920s.

Remington is one of America's oldest gunmakers and one of the largest U.S. producers of shotguns and rifles. The company was founded in 1816 by Eliphalet Remington in upstate New York. Today, Remington operates plants in Kentucky and Arkansas, but the original firearms plant and custom shop is still located in Ilion, N Y

IT MAY NOT BE THE HILTON

This hunter's cabin is in need of a little repair work, but it's surely the perfect size for a small group of hunters. If properly cared for, a solid log structure like this could serve many generations of deer hunters. Photo circa 1901.

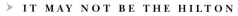

HOME AWAY FROM HOME

Five stalwart Norwegian hunters pose in front of their sturdy log cabin in the wilds of northern Minnesota. Between them, they are wielding two Winchester lever-action rifles and two Remington Model 8 semiautomatic rifles, perfect medicine for Minnesota whitetails. Photo by W.T. Oxley, courtesy of Richard Oxley.

A SNUG CABIN IN THE WOODS

Smoke billows out of the chimney of this log cabin indicating that a number of happy hunters are warm and cozy inside. Outside, the fruits of their labor clearly weigh down a stout buck pole, the results of several days in the woods. Leaning against the wooden ladder next to the cabin are two of the hunters' rifles, the one on the left being a semiautomatic Remington Model 8. The photo is believed to have been taken in Upper Michigan, circa 1910 to 1915.

IT'LL DO IN A PINCH

Talk about a basic shelter. The log entrance looks more like an old mine shaft built into the side of the hill, and much like the sod houses settlers used on the Great Plains in the 1870s and '80s. Let's hope it is warm, dry and spacious inside. The warmly dressed hunter in this aged cabinet photo is posing with a tang-sighted Winchester Model 94 rifle across his lap. Two Marlin lever-action rifles are leaning on the logs behind him, indicating at least three venturesome hunters are using this primitive abode. Photo circa 1915.

DEER CAMP CHARACTERS

▲ **BOUNTY FOR THE CHEF**

This classic photo is well composed and has a great deal happening in it. With a spike buck and a doe hanging, along with two raccoons, the knife-wielding chef is ready to demonstrate his culinary skills for this congenial group of hunters. Young and old, they all have a role to play at the camp. In the late 1800s and early 1900s, eating was almost as important as hunting, and it was not unusual for larger deer camps to hire a chef for the week.

The men are holding an assortment of meat-getting firearms: side-by-side shotguns, Winchester lever-action rifles – including one Model 1895 in the foreground, and at least one Marlin lever action. This outstanding camp photo could have been taken in any number of states from Pennsylvania to Minnesota. Photo circa 1910.

THE WEATHER IS BREAKING – TIME TO HEAD TO THE WOODS

The snow has finally stopped and after being confined to the tents for many long hours, several of the men in camp, including the cook and faithful dog, step outside to get some fresh air and have a smoke. Several deer hooves from a deer already processed hang on the meat pole. Time's a wasting. Better grab a rifle and head to that favorite deer crossing before daylight's gone. Photo circa 1910.

A TYPICAL GROUP OF GOOD-OL'-BOY DEER HUNTERS

These 1950s-era hunters, who are all firemen from New York state, are having a great time in deer camp and it shows. With their checkered mackinaws, their Winchester rifles and plenty of ammunition, they're headed out to their stands for the afternoon's adventure. Photo taken in the Adirondacks, circa early 1950s.

⋀ OFF TO A GOOD START

These grinning characters have gotten off to a fine start. Judging by the assortment of arms they are brandishing, they should have no problem adding to the buck pole by the end of the week. The man on the left is holding a Remington Model 8 and the man next to him has what looks like a Winchester lever-action rifle with a side-mounted scope. The man in the middle has a bolt-action rifle, while the man standing next to him poses with a semiauto Winchester Model 1907, and the happy hunter on the far right has a celebratory beverage in one hand and his shotgun in the other. Photo circa 1925.

⋖ CANADIAN ADVENTURE

This rough-and-tumble group of white-tail characters was photographed near Orillia, Ontario, Canada, in the late 1930s or early '40s. They look determined and ready to handle any challenges that may come their way.

➤ A PINT-SIZE CABIN

As long as the hunting is good, these three successful hunters don't seem to mind the fact that this tiny trapper's cabin might get rather crowded. The three deer tied to the roof logs are proof enough that hunting in the area must be very good, indeed. Plenty of venison makes cramped quarters a bit easier to handle. Photo circa 1920.

▽ ONE HAPPY FAMILY OF HUNTERS

These five Massachusetts hunters have just returned to Boston from the Big Woods of Maine with their venison prize. The back of the photo reads: "Dad, Lawrence and Grampie." Dad, on left, may be getting a hug from his son. Lawrence and Grampie are kneeling in the foreground and their pal leans against the car's fender. Photo dated 1945.

▲ LOCKED AND LOADED

These four veteran buck hunters are loaded down with guns and gear – ready to strike a trail in the backcountry and spend a few glorious days chasing magnificent whitetails. Note the Adirondack basket, a popular method of packing gear in the 1920s and '30s. Taken in the Northeast, the photo is dated 1938.

➤ HAROLD AND HIS HUNTERS

This motley group of happy-go-lucky deer hunters hails from West Virginia. The back of the photo reads: "Harold and deer hunting party, 1950s." No doubt this bunch of characters has plenty of tall tales to tell from deer camp.

POWER IS TOPS

PETERS "HIGH VELOCITY" ▶
BIG GAME CARTRIDGE
with "INNER-BELTED"
soft-point bullet.

"There's no more powerful ammunition in the world than PETERS 'HIGH VELOCITY'!"

says "DOC" PETERS

PETERS CARTRIDGE DIVISION, *Remington Arms Company, Inc., Bridgeport 2, Conn.—"High Velocity" is Reg. U. S. Pat. Off. "Inner-Belted" is a trade mark of Peters Cartridge Division.*

"POWER IS WHAT YOU WANT in the ammunition you buy! And POWER is the reason so many hunters prefer Peters 'High Velocity' big game cartridges. They have *extra* power for all hunting ranges to bring down medium and big game. Peters 'Inner-Belted' bullets provide terrific impact without disintegrating. They expand uniformly, give maximum knockdown power. 'Inner-Belted' soft-point and hollow-point bullets available in popular calibers. Center-fire cartridges also supplied with metal case bullets, protected point expanding bullets and regular soft-point and lead bullets for selected calibers. Ask your dealer for Peters 'High Velocity'! Size for size — for any standard center-fire rifle *there's no more powerful big game ammunition in the world!"*

Send a dime, your name and address for a copy of the 48-page booklet "How To Dress, Ship and Cook Wild Game."

PETERS
PACKS THE POWER
DUPONT

GETTIN' 'EM OUT, TRAVOIS STYLE

While World War I is raging in France, some enterprising New England hunters have had themselves a whale of a day. What better way to get their three deer out of the woods than to borrow a time-honored method from the Plains Indians and build themselves a travois to haul out their prize, including one real whopper of a buck with at least a 20-inch spread. The bridge is made out of hand-cut logs. The veteran workhorse is looking back as if to say, "Okay, boys, enough of this picture taking. Let's get these critters back to the barn so I can relax." Photo from Salem, Mass., circa 1918.

> As to getting deer out of the woods, a horse is a real joy. A big buck is hard to carry any other way and heavy to drag unless you have four or five men and a tow rope. But it's better to drag him than to try to carry him on a single pole unless you have a short way to go and a number of men to help, as you may have when driving deer. This much-used method is an abomination. The deer swings back and forth. The weight of the pole makes the load heavier and the pole cuts the shoulder. No, I am not for this pole method with two men at all.

John Madson, 1961
From *The White-Tailed Deer*, published by the Conservation Department of Olin Mathieson Chemical Company, East Alton, Illinois.

CHAPTER 7

GETTIN' 'EM OUT

The common adage, "Deer hunting is a lot of fun until you shoot something; that's when the real work begins," easily could have originated a century ago. The task of transporting a 200-plus-pound carcass out of the woods back then was perhaps a much greater challenge than it is today because of wilderness settings, poor roads and limited access. With the advent of snowmobiles, four-wheel drive trucks and all-terrain vehicles, and easier access to most areas we hunt across America these days, we often can drive right up to our deer and load them in the back. But, it wasn't always that simple.

Just like today, deer hunters of yesteryear were highly innovative. When the going got tough – and it usually was – they devised countless ways to make the job easier. By far, though, it often boiled down to muscles and shoe leather with a bunch of determination thrown in for good measure. There was one major difference. Our rugged forefathers were used to hard work and they welcomed the challenge; it was part of the experience. Once back at camp, as venison chops were sizzling on the stove, a man could sit back in front of a crackling fire, sip on a well-earned dose of blizzard medicine, and reflect. Life was good!

As you'll see, some of the methods to the madness included single horses, horse-drawn wagons, horse- or ox-drawn sleds when deep snow covered the ground, hand-drawn sleds, motorcycles, railroads, canoes, bateaus or other boats, Indian-style travois, the single "he-man" over-the-shoulder method, the two-man-and-a-pole method so disliked by William Monypeny Newsom, makeshift stretchers, and by far the most common – one or more men simply taking turns dragging a buck out of the woods. Of course, as the 20th century progressed, automobiles and trucks also played an ever-expanding role in getting deer out of the woods.

Abraham Lincoln once said that a fire warms you three different ways: the first by the exertion of cutting the wood, the second by being exposed to the heat of a fire, and the third by the warm feeling of satisfaction a man gets from sitting in front of the mesmerizing flames. Likewise, a true deer hunter gets an indescribable sense of satisfaction in making a good shot, investing a little "sweat equity" in getting his buck out of the woods and back to camp, and later being able to admire the fruits of his labor as his trophy hangs proudly on the buck pole. With deer hunting, there is also a fourth and extremely important dynamic – the delight one receives from enjoying all of that delicious venison long after the hunt has ended.

3814   Only another mile to camp.

⋏ PADDLING QUIETLY BACK TO CAMP

This content but alert hunter already has a grand supply of meat, but he knows he can't be too careful as he paddles silently down a backwater through the North Country in his birch bark canoe. His always dependable lever-action rifle is balanced across the gunwales in front of him, just in case a big ol' buck appears on the edge of the woods, he wants to be ready to jump into action at a moment's notice. With two large does in the front of the canoe, one has to wonder what it would be like to trade places with him as he glides along through the snowy wilderness wonderland around him. Titled "Only another mile to camp." This vintage stereoview was published by The Universal Photo Art Co. of Philadelphia, Pa., in the late 1880s.

➤ A WALK IN THE WOODS

When all else fails, a good walking stick for balance and some strong muscles and shoe leather always seems to work in a pinch on a cold snowy day in the North Country. After the effort these two hunters have exerted to get their buck out of the woods, they'll surely savor the backstraps they plan to rustle up for supper back at camp. The second hunter is toting a trusty Savage Model 99. The picture could have been taken anywhere from Maine to Minnesota, but one thing is certain – with the emotional high these two are on, they definitely are not suffering from the cold. Dated Nov. 11, 1903.

A STRONG BACK AND DOGGED DETERMINATION

Arriving back in camp with a fine doe strapped under his arm and his trusty Remington Model 14 pump firmly by his side, this determined hunter is having no difficulty carrying his load. Judging by the vintage automobiles in the background, the photo was taken between 1915 and 1920. No location is given, but this scene has been played out a million times in a million bustling deer camps across America.

THE LONG TREK HOME

In this 1888 B.W. Kilburn stereoview taken in New England and titled, "Homeward Bound," two weary hunters plod through the snow after a long day afield. The tall man on the left heaves a large doe over his shoulder, while the bearded old-timer to his left holds an ancient muzzleloader, a folded deer skin, a large raccoon pelt and a fox skin draped over his shoulder. It's been a good day, but they'll be glad to reach the cabin, eat some vittles and rest their weary bones in front of a warm fire.

JAMES M. DAVIS, New York, St. Louis, Liverpool, Toronto, Sydney.

Copyright 1888 by B. W. Kilburn

4976. Homeward Bound.

Floating the Buck to Camp.
Copyright, 1893, by Geo. Barker.

FLOATING THE BUCK TO CAMP

With their knives, belt hatchets and brace of lever-action rifles leaning in the front of the bateau, and their long wooden oars, these two seasoned whitetail hunters will have no problem maneuvering this massive 9-point buck back to camp. And what a head full of bone! The buck's body almost takes up the entire boat. Wearing hip boots and smiling confidently, these hardy outdoorsmen know how to get around in the backwater country of New England. Dated 1893, the stereoview was published by Underwood and Underwood. Photo by George Barker.

BROTHERLY LOVE

Next to physically dragging a buck out of the woods, tying it to a stout pole was probably the most widely used method of removing a deer from the woods early in the 20th century. Two strong hunters could share the load by lashing a deer to the pole and each holding one end. Here, brothers George and Ralph Haley carry a young 8-point buck to the barn after a successful morning's hunt. Both brothers are hunting with classic 1893 Marlin lever-action repeaters; the long gun on the left sports a saddle ring while the gun on the right has a half magazine. Photo circa early 1900s.

RETURNING TO CAMP

HIGHLANDS OF CANADA

2090 S

▲ GETTING THE JOB DONE

It's a good thing these men are young and strong. In the Canadian bush, two young hunters are doing it the hard way, returning to camp with six deer and a canoe between them. The does and yearlings are lighter and much easier to throw over a shoulder, but that big 10-pointer might be a different story. The photo is from a printed postcard dated 1907. The caption reads: "Returning to Camp, Highlands of Canada."

▶ SOMEWHERE IN THE WILDS OF CANADA

Toting their reliable Winchesters, these two wool-clad hunters have their work cut out for them as they carry a fine 10-point buck back to camp somewhere in the wilds of Canada. Youthful, strong and determined, they don't seem to mind the labor. With a prize like this, who could complain? Photo circa 1910.

DEER-SHOOTING, CANADA

The makeshift stretcher seems somewhat awkward, but with a prize like this, it'll be well worth the work when these men finally reach camp! The rifle in the foreground is an early pump action. In case the nice 8-pointer gets too heavy, the hunting buddy sitting on the right can lend a hand with the transporting. Photo postcard circa 1910.

Courtesy Hoppe's.

▲ EVERYONE LENDS A HAND

Part of the camaraderie of deer camp is helping a fellow hunter find his deer and get it back to camp. It certainly appears as though this pipe-smoking crew is willing and able to do just that. At least half the camp has turned out to admire this fine young buck, taken with an ever-dependable Remington Model 8. Could these men have other motives? Could they be secretly licking their chops at the thought of sharing some tender and delicious venison roast soon to be simmering over the fire? Photo circa 1915.

For the Great Army of Deer Hunters!

Maybe it's that crafty old Blacktail buck, napping in the Alders . . . or the shy, elusive Whitetail, ready to hoist his white flag and vanish, phantom-like, in the forest, at the slightest warning. But wherever, whatever the species of deer you hunt, the new Savage Model 99RS—the "Ideal Deer Rifle", and the new .250/3000 cartridge with 100 grain hollow point bullet, will provide shooting satisfaction you've never known before.

The New "Ideal Deer Rifle"

Light to carry—quick to handle—easy to shoot from any position, the Model 99RS embodies all the popular characteristics of the "99", a hammerless, solid breech, lever action repeating rifle, famous for 30 years. These new and noteworthy features have been incorporated:

Barrel especially selected for accuracy and made from Savage Hi-Pressure Steel. Nicely tapered of medium weight and fitted with raised ramp front sight base. Special design large full pistol grip stock and forearm of selected walnut, handsomely checkered, oil finish. Steel butt plate of shotgun design. Lyman Windgauge and Elevation adjustment rear peep sight; Lyman folding leaf middle and gold bead front

sight. Equipped with ⅞" military type leather sling strap with quick release swivels and screw studs. Weight about 7½ lbs. Calibers .250/3000 and .300. *Retail price, complete,* Model 99RS . . $71.50.

This rifle is furnished without sling strap with semi-buckhorn rear and gold bead front sights—also in .303 caliber. Model 99R. *Retail price, complete* . . . $52.80.

Other styles of Model 99 rifles from $41.25
The quality combination—Savage
Rifles—Savage Ammunition

SAVAGE
ARMS CORPORATION, UTICA, NEW YORK
Manufacturers of Savage, Stevens and A. H. Fox Sporting Arms

$17.95 WINCHESTER RIFLES—Model 92; Cal. 44/40
20" bbl.—Carbine $33.35 List;
Special $17.95

WINCHESTER **Model 57**: Rechambered; Cal. 22 Long Rifle; $31.65 List; Special..$17.95
WINCHESTER **Model 55**: take-down; 25-35; 30-30; 32 Spl.; brand new, shipped in orginal
    sealed packages. List $44.70; Special $26.50. Ammunition for Model 55's—per 100—$5.00
REMINGTON **Mod. 29 Pump Gun**: 12 gauge only; all lengths; $37.10 list; Special.................$26.50
REMINGTON **Mod. 17**: 20 gauge only; standard lengths; $37.10 list; Special......................$26.50

SLOANS SPORTING GOODS CO.,   **N-88 Chambers Street**   **NEW YORK CITY**

⌃ **PRESERVING THE MEMORY**

These two proud hunters have good reason to be smiling with two tremendous bucks strapped to the fenders of their automobile transport. Parked in front of the photography studio of A.M. Turnquist in Duluth, Minn., they had the good sense to capture the memory of their incredible hunt on film. Who wouldn't want to have a keepsake of these two Minnesota brutes? Axel M. Turnquist, or "A.M." as he was locally known, was a popular Swedish-American photographer who lived and worked in the Duluth area from the mid-1890s to the early 1920s. Photo circa 1920.

SOME HELPFUL HORSEPOWER

This successful hunter is fortunate to have the help of a stout and dependable workhorse to pack his spike buck out to the camp. Horses not accustomed to the smell of blood or not used to carrying a dead animal will often shy away from such a task. The beautiful Marlin rifle with tang sights and diamond inlay on the fore-end is a Model 1894 with a half magazine.

ONLY A HUNTER CAN EXPLAIN

Avid whitetail hunter J.A. Plummer obviously relished the outdoor life. Probably shot the afternoon before, the doe he is carrying is frozen solid. On the back of the Nov. 12, 1924, photo, Mr. Plummer wrote the following:

"This the Prize, to bring in our deer, to get one of these out and bring it to camp is a satisfaction and a pleasure that only a hunter can explain."
Initials "JAP" for J.A. Plummer

Written under Mr. Plummer's inscription, someone else added: "Plummer sure loved hunting, especially ducks."

THE BEST OF BOTH WORLDS

Who needs four wheels when you can ride a Harley? Showing off his outstanding trophy 10-point buck, this innovative 1930s hunter has the best of both worlds. He can ride his Harley deep into the snowy backcountry where automobiles dare not tread, and he can easily get his trophy buck out of the woods in the sidecar. Photo circa 1930.

A NEW JERSEY
ADRENALINE RUSH

Paul Schmidt and James Benson, who hail from Elmer, N.J., manhandle a hefty 8-pointer out of the woods
on opening day of the New Jersey season in December
1937. Both men were members of the Indian Mills Gun
Club. The historic club is still in existence today.

⍦ THE CALL OF THE WILD

There is something timelessly exhilarating about paddling a canoe in a lake or stream in the backcountry, quietly cutting through the glassy water while scanning every inch of the adjoining shoreline for a hidden buck. The glint of an antler, the flick of an ear, a body part that appears out of place in the brush – these are the telltale clues that a veteran woodsman quickly notices. This lucky young hunter has hit a home run. He can barely fit into his canoe with the load he's carrying – but he's probably not grumbling. The buck is enormous! The printed postcard photo comes from Stoney Lake in Ontario, Canada, circa 1930.

⌃ WHITETAIL GOLD MINE IN CANADA

American deer hunter Norman Paget (front) and his Ontario guide negotiate a big-bodied 8-pointer taken near Huntsville and Algonquin Provincial Park on opening day of the 1940 season. Since many Canadian sportsmen were already in uniform and participating in that seemingly far-off war in Europe, American hunters like Paget had a field day traveling to Canada in the late 1930s and early '40s. In those days, it was an easy matter to get firearms across the border, and American dollars were always welcome. Of course, no one could have known that the U.S. would be entering that terrible war, courtesy of Japan, in just over one year's time. Note the rifle resting on the buck's chest as they haul it out to camp.

Those Were The Days

BY ARCHIBALD RUTLEDGE

> **MORE THAN ONE WAY TO GET 'ER DONE**
With pipe in his mouth, this smiling hunter is doing it the easy way, sledding his hefty and half-frozen 6-point buck into camp on a homemade wooden sled. The photo is from the 1920s or '30s at a well-established "Down East" deer camp.

IF RIFLES COULD TALK...

The classic Savage Model 99 in the foreground, caressed fondly by the old-timer wearing a vest and tie, could likely tell some spellbinding stories of frosty mornings and rutting bucks of days gone by. The rifle definitely adds to the mood as four wool-clad woodsmen, each with a trusty firearm at their side, proudly show off a bounty of five large-bodied deer on a sagging meat pole. Note the two bucks on the right and the spike on the left are wearing tags, but the does are not. The photo was taken in Wisconsin or Minnesota in the early 1900s.

" **The whitetail deer is now, and we hope always will be, the big game of the common man. The machine operator and the office worker, the small businessman and the farmer, share equal opportunities to return with the spoils of a deer hunt. Perhaps in no other way is this better exemplified than in the taking of outstanding whitetail trophies. Most often it is the man of comfortable wealth, the hunter with ample funds and time to spare, who hunts for and bags the largest trophies of other species – moose, elk, caribou, mountain sheep and bear. But most of the prize whitetail heads adorn the homes of the butcher, the baker and the candlestick maker.** "

Lawrence R. Koller
Shots at Whitetails, 1948

CHAPTER 8

THE ICONIC BUCK POLE

Every deer camp of yesteryear had its very own version of a buck pole. Somehow it seems difficult for the human brain to conjure up an image of an empty picturesque deer camp at the end of a week of dedicated hunting. Although hunters certainly did get "skunked" from time to time, few – if any – photographs were ever taken of a buck pole standing bare and empty. However, fully laden with six bucks, eight bucks, four bucks, or any number of bucks, does and maybe a bear or two with an occasional moose thrown in after scouring the woods for days or even weeks, the buck pole is suddenly transformed into something quite extraordinary. It became a thing of beauty to be admired by all, a unique shrine dedicated to an amazing animal that represented the sum total of time and sacrifice that has gone into the enterprise. Why? Because even in a lifeless state, whitetails are the most beautiful and majestic creatures in the world.

Once a meat pole – or skinning pole or buck pole – was filled to the brim with deer, something magical always occurred. For a brief and fleeting moment, time seemed to stand still as men stared at the fruits of their labor, showing great respect for such a worthy adversary, admiring and proudly pointing to their trophies and sharing a few tall tales about the hunt. Even though there was much work yet to do – skinning carcasses and butchering many pounds of savory venison – no one was overly anxious to undo what had been done. The contents of the buck pole symbolized the essence of why these men had left their warm homes, traveled to the wilderness, and collectively braved the elements to accomplish a common goal and seek a little adventure along the way.

The meat pole was a badge of honor representing every facet of a memorable hunt. As soon as it was filled to capacity with hanging carcasses, it was understandable that it would remain a sacred shrine for as long as possible; the colder the weather, the better. No hunter worth his salt would ever allow the spoilage of any meat.

Likewise, no man in camp ever wanted to dismantle a fully laden buck pole. But, alas, the moment would have to come when the work of cutting up meat must begin. Although it was work, butchering deer was not altogether an unpleasant task. However, something was definitely lost when the buck pole once again stood bare and empty and everyone felt those deep pangs of sorrow. Much of the joy and magic of deer camp was somehow gone. Fortunately, thousands upon thousands of photographs of this sacred shrine were taken that survive to this day, helping to forever capture those special moments.

NOTHING LIKE THE SWEET SMELL OF SUCCESS

The caption on this postcard reads: "A Three Day's Deer Hunt, near Stanley, Wis. Published for Phillips Studio." Stanley is just east of Eau Claire in the central part of the state. Judging by the sheer number of deer hanging from the pole, it must have been a very productive three days for these seven laid-back hunters. Now it's time to enjoy the mild weather and take a well-deserved midday siesta. The surrounding cutover area obviously has become prime whitetail habitat, one of the few fringe benefits of clearcutting the vast virgin forests of the upper Midwest. Circa 1900.

SQUIRREL STEW TONIGHT

These two hardy woodsmen have plenty to be happy about. In addition to a pair of fine antlered bucks hanging on the pole, they have bagged an assortment of small game, mostly squirrels, but a rabbit or two as well. The man on the left is holding a Model 1895 Winchester while his cohort is wielding a long-barrel Winchester lever-action rifle. The photo is somewhat out of focus, probably due to being made on a time-lapse glass negative. Photo circa early 1900s.

DIXIELAND DEER HUNT

Judging by the relatively small body sizes of the hanging deer, including one nice buck on the far right, and the southern loblolly pines in the background, this old cabinet photo was taken somewhere in the Deep South. After a spectacular morning, these relaxed hunters are giving the deer a midday break. A buckboard, a large black dog and part of a tent also appear in the background, indicating the group is in a cozy southern deer camp. It's likely these men are hunting with dogs. Circa early 1900s.

FATHER AND SON DEER HUNT

An apparent father and son pose for the camera with their sure-shooting, long-barrel lever-action rifles and the prizes of a successful hunt. The father (left) is leaning on his trusty Marlin Model 1893 while his son holds a meat-getting Winchester '94. The buck in the center, an exceptional 10-pointer, is enormous, likely weighing in excess of 250 pounds. Photo circa early 1900s.

⌃ C'EST SI BON! VIVE LE CANADA!

From a printed postcard titled "Scenes of Canadian Life," and postmarked April 1906, Clinton, Ontario, these accomplished hunters have accounted for many meals of venison, and some very good racks as displayed on a very long and sagging buck pole. The hunt probably took place in the fall of 1905. Since most of the men are wearing similar hats and sweaters, they are likely French-Canadians. Most of the visible rifles appear to be lever actions, and a canoe and lake can be seen in the background behind the hanging deer. C'est si Bon!

⌃ HANG 'EM HIGH

Twenty-two-year-old Charles Niblett proudly poses with his Winchester rifle as he stands by a buck pole containing one thick-necked mature buck, one mature doe and two yearling fawns. The photo was taken in November 1906 near Finlayson, Minn., in Pine County. A handwritten inscription on the back of the photo reads, "Frank Fox cabin near Chisley Brook. We could shoot three deer then." Located in east-central Minnesota, Pine County borders Wisconsin.

SOME SERIOUS ANTLERS

Several bruiser bucks weigh down this sagging meat pole as these four turn-of-the-century hunters and a blurry dog on the right display an impressive array of venison and firepower. The man on the left has a Remington Autoloading Rifle – later known as the legendary Model 8 – while his cohort has a Winchester carbine. Judging by his bullet belt, the Winchester man won't be running out of ammunition any time soon. The hunter on the far right is armed with a popular Winchester 1895 while his partner has a tang-sighted Model 94 Winchester lever action. The photo postcard was made between 1910 and 1915.

▼ YOU CAN'T GO WRONG WITH A MODEL 8

Mature bucks are never easy to bring down, but judging by their success, these hunters know their way around the deer woods. Four of the six bucks hanging boast bragging size headgear, while four of the six snow-powdered hunters are wielding ever-popular Remington Model 8 rifles. John Browning certainly hit a home run with his enduring Model 8. Originally brought out as the Remington Autoloading Rifle in 1906, the name was changed to the Remington Model 8 in 1911. As the first semiautomatic rifle made intentionally for sport hunting and offered in a number of versatile calibers, the rifle proved enormously popular across North America for all types of big game, especially burly whitetails.

◄ THE ESSENCE OF TRANQUILITY

While the bucks are not gigantic, this dreamy photograph tells a special story because of the mood it creates. You have to wonder where that misty dirt road leads. Five content hunters, five bucks hanging and five classic deer rifles suggest the makings of a memorable few days in deer camp. From left to right the men are holding: a Savage Model 99, a Winchester lever action, a .30-40 Krag-Jorgenson, and two more reliable lever-action Winchesters. One can easily imagine a scene like this in a Pennsylvania deer camp in the late 1920s or early '30s. Due to the peaceful nature of the photo, perhaps we could call it "Camp Tranquility."

NO. 4998

DEER HUNTING,
BESSEMER, MICH.

▲ BUCKS ON THE RIGHT, DOES ON THE LEFT

Someone took great care in arranging the 17 deer seen in this color postcard so that the resulting photograph would be picture perfect. Printed around 1910, the photo was taken near Bessemer, Mich. Does whitetail hunting get any better than this?

➤ FOR EVERYTHING THERE IS A SEASON

The snow has stopped falling, another grand hunt has ended. The time has come to reflect and be thankful. Grasping his Winchester rifle, avid whitetail hunter Carl Merrow of Bigelow, Maine, is doing just that. Photo circa 1910.

MAKING MEMORIES IN THE DEEP WOODS

(1) A deep-woods tent camp and two bucks hanging sets the mood for this pipe-smoking lad as he proudly holds onto his Remington pump Model 14 and stands next to the buck that probably fell to his rifle. A good tracking snow on the ground no doubt contributed to his success.

(2) At the opposite end of the buck pole, another pipe-smoking young man dressed in mechanic's coveralls proudly stands next to the fine buck that he downed with his long-barrel, tang-sighted Winchester.

➤ BUCK POLE MEMORIES

With five deer hanging including three very nice bucks, the hunters who have set up camp in this snow-covered section of woods must be having the time of their lives. There is nothing quite like the sweet smell of success. The chimney coming out of the large wall tent in the background shows that the hunters inside will remain cozy and happy. Although this photo was taken about 85 years ago, it could easily be an American scene from last hunting season. Photo circa 1930s.

▲ CAMP BUCKTAIL, 1923

Pictured with 11 fine bucks, these nine deer-slayers seem to take their success quite seriously – notice the jokester above the buck pole. No locale is given, and Camp Bucktail could be just about anywhere from Maine to Minnesota. But judging from the body sizes and impressive antlers of the deer, Camp Bucktail might well have been located in northern Minnesota or Wisconsin. There is a "Bucktail Lane" near Rhinelander, Wis., and the road name could have come from an old deer camp as Rhinelander lies in the heart of prime deer country.

The Name "Bucktail" is also quite common in Pennsylvania, so Camp Bucktail could have been located somewhere in the Pocono Mountains. Wherever this camp of yesteryear was, it no doubt created some fine memories.

THE HISTORIC PENNSYLVANIA BUCKTAILS

During the Civil War, members of the 13th Pennsylvania Reserves customarily wore a piece of a bucktail pinned to their caps. Thus they became widely known as the "Pennsylvania Bucktails." A bucktail also hung on the company flagstaff. Most of the men who served in the 13th were rugged, rough-and-tumble backwoodsmen from logging camps and sawmills and frequently hunted deer for food. As experienced hunters, they were very proud of their shooting skills. The Bucktails saw considerable action in Virginia in 1862, and later earned distinction as brave fighters and sharpshooters at the decisive Battle of Gettysburg.

▼ LUCKY THIRTEEN

What a range of firearms. With four deer hanging in the background, this photogenic group of hunters has certainly produced some venison, but with such a wide array of rifles and scatterguns, one has to wonder what methods were used to find success. Were these men engaged in several organized drives? The shotguns could be European, indicating an ethnic group. Could they be Italian? The dapper, pipe-smoking young man on the left with the holstered pistol could almost be a double for a young Leonardo DiCaprio who has just stepped off a Hollywood set. And the old-timer next to him is wielding a short old Winchester Trapper's Carbine. How about that for a meat rifle! Photo circa 1930.

▶ FIVE MEN, FIVE DEER

A picturesque winter wonderland reveals a sturdy meat pole holding four yearling bucks and one large-antlered buck. The pipe-smoking hunter on the left is leaning on his classic Remington Model 8. His cohort on the far right sports a Winchester. Can we assume that each of these hunters accounted for one of the bucks? Photo circa 1930.

▲ **IS THIS WHITETAIL HEAVEN?**

This happy deer hunter has a lot to contemplate as he stands next to a heavily laden buck pole with a thick-necked bull-of-the-woods nearly touching the ground. With his dependable Remington Model 8 rifle, a good skinning knife in his belt, an aromatic pipe in his mouth and a cozy cabin only a few feet away, this could be the true definition of whitetail heaven.

◄ Showing off a holstered Model 1911 .45 Colt automatic in his belt, this sophisticated companion obviously enjoys posing for the camera. Could that be his thick antlered 8-point buck hanging on the pole? Photos circa 1925.

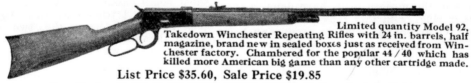

Courtesy Winchester Repeating Arms.

⌃ WELCOME TO SWALLOW FALLS INN

This old photo makes you want to sit down on the porch and share a cold Orange Crush with this jovial bunch. In its day, Swallow Falls Inn must have been a popular destination for deer hunters from Maryland, Pennsylvania and West Virginia. Located in western Maryland near Oakland and the Youghiogheny River close to the West Virginia state line, the deer were never known to be exceptionally large in this rugged country – but no one seemed to mind.

Judging from the smiling faces, not to mention the six bucks hanging on the porch, these hunters are enjoying themselves immensely. If we were in a time machine, we could drink a couple of sodas while filling up with Conoco leaded gasoline at about 15 cents per gallon. The man and

two ladies standing on the porch are likely the owners or managers of the Inn. It's a safe bet that most of these beaming deer hunters hail from the Pittsburgh area. What a smorgasbord of classic whitetail rifles they have among them!

As one might expect, a number of Winchesters are in the mix. At least one Remington Model 14 pump action sits in the middle of the front row, and two military-style bolt-action rifles can be seen on the right that appear to be Springfield Armory .30-40 Krags. The rifle on the far right is a variation of the veritable Marlin Model 1893 lever action with a straight stock. Say what you want, but this jolly crew proves that the golden days of deer hunting were a mighty fine time to be alive. Photo circa 1930.

⌃ RIFLES AT REST

A fine array of rifle hardware accompanies this Michigan buck pole filled with a half-dozen prime bucks. Photo taken near Iron Mountain, Mich., in 1940 by L.L. Cook.

➤ WHAT A HUNT

After all the smoke clears and all is said and done, it matters little whether one buck hangs in camp or 20; the feeling of satisfaction hunters get when they see and admire their buck hanging on the pole is like nothing else in the world. Central North Carolina, circa 1940.

A GOOD DOG, A GOOD RIFLE AND A GOOD BUCK
The driver of the 1920s vintage flatbed truck smiles through the back window as the older man in the back holds his dog and poses for the camera. The long-barrel Winchester could be a Model 1886, 1892 or 1894, all very successful deer rifles. Photo circa early1920s.

" My new repeater. Fifteen shots, almost any one of which would have got the game had I but one shot. Speed of fire is a good servant, but a bad master. "

Theodore S. Van Dyke
The Still-Hunter, 1882

CHAPTER 9

GUNS THAT WON THE EAST

In the decades following the Civil War, whitetail hunting in America underwent a considerable transition from sustenance and market hunting to sport hunting. Hunters were still going after meat as a primary objective, but the challenge and thrill of deer hunting became a much-loved form of outdoor recreation for many Americans. Sportsmen from big cities in the east traveled to the Adirondacks and northern Maine to pursue their passion for whitetail hunting. Likewise, sportsmen traveled to the North Country of Minnesota and Wisconsin for the same reason.

The rapid development of new firearms made primarily for military purposes both during and after the Civil War coincided perfectly with America's newfound passion for deer and big-game hunting in general. It was only natural that hunters would begin to use some of the newer weapons as tools of their trade. In the late 1800s and early 1900s, the transition from antiquated hand-me-down muzzleloaders to the new generation of lever-action and semiautomatic hunting rifles occurred swiftly as it followed an ever-expanding country that steadily spread its wings in a westward direction. Whereas many of the early Henry and Winchester repeating rifles of the 1860s and '70s were being used in the West for self-preservation against hostile Indians, Easterners quickly

realized the benefits of adopting these guns for deer, bear, moose and caribou.

Seeing the great potential for this new market, manufacturers began to design and build rifles especially for sport hunting purposes. The transition was particularly rapid in the Northeast where many of the revolutionary new guns were being made. Winchester Repeating Arms Co. was founded in New Haven, Conn., in 1866. Marlin Firearms Co. of North Haven, Conn., followed a few years later in 1870. Remington Arms was founded in upstate New York.

Hunters were anxious to get the newest and best the market had to offer. This trend spread rapidly to the Midwest, especially in the big deer country of northern Michigan, Minnesota and Wisconsin. The transition was a little slower in more remote and poorer economic regions like West Virginia, Kentucky and the southern Appalachians. Old ways died hard in the mountain regions. Pre-Civil War muzzleloaders and shotguns, some of which had been converted from flintlocks to percussion guns years earlier, were passed down from generation to generation. By the early 1900s, many an old mountaineer was still using the same long rifle his father had used for deer. Congressional Medal of Honor winner Alvin York of Tennessee grew up shooting a vintage, hand-me-down, single-shot muzzleloader, a gun with which he reportedly could shoot the head off a turkey at 50 yards.

Winchester lever-action rifles became enormously popular for deer and moose in the Northeast where they were made. The venerable Model '94 Winchester lever action eventually became the most popular deer rifle America had ever seen. Its popularity quickly spread throughout the country. Marlin lever-action rifles were also extremely popular. Marlin certainly gave Winchester a run for its money by making its own style of tough and reliable rifles, but Marlin repeaters never enjoyed the immense popularity of the Winchester '94, which became "America's deer rifle." Other models like the Winchester 1895 – the first of its kind to feature a box magazine – became favorites among whitetail and big-game hunters across the nation as well.

Next to the Winchesters and Marlins, the hammerless, lever-action Savage Model 1899, originally offered with a rotary magazine, became a gun of choice for thousands of avid hunters. The early 1900s saw the debut of the Winchester Model 1907, with a detachable box magazine, and the Remington Model 8, which came with a fixed magazine, the first semiautomatic rifles made specifically with sportsmen in mind. A few years later, Remington introduced the pump-action Model 14. These four classic rifles also became huge favorites with whitetail hunters.

Bolt-action military rifles made in the late 19th century were also adopted by whitetail hunters. One of the most popular, the Springfield Armory Krag-Jorgensen, made from 1892 to 1899, became quite common in big-game camps across the nation. Carbine and sporterized versions were highly prized by many hunters.

From about 1907 to 1920, bolt-action, pump and semiautomatic rifles and cartridges targeted especially for deer hunters saw an ever-expanding market. These rifles, along with the old original classics – the Winchester and Marlin lever-action repeaters, the Savage 99, and later the Winchester 1907, the Remington Model 8 and the Remington Model 14, will always be the guns that won the Eastern deer woods.

◄ A FINE SPECIMEN

Both older men standing beside this thick-necked buck are armed with popular Springfield Armory .30-40 Krag-Jorgensen rifles. The man to the left of the deer holds a military-style Krag with a full stock, while his companion on the right holds a carbine or sporterized version. The .30-40 Gov't., or .30 Army, was the first smokeless powder cartridge adopted by the U.S. government. The Krag's unique side-mounted hinge magazine and slick-working bolt action made it a favorite of American big-game hunters for many years. Only one member of this quartet has bragging rights to a well-placed shot on this brute of a whitetail. Who do you think it is? Photo circa 1915 to 1920.

A BUDDING PRESIDENT

Like many avid big-game hunters in the late 1800s, legendary outdoorsman Theodore Roosevelt was a Winchester man through and through. During his ranching days in North Dakota in the mid 1880s, he owned and used at least three Model 1876 lever-action Winchesters with which he hunted a variety of big game – a carbine and rifle chambered in .40-60 W.C.F. and a rifle chambered in .45-75. He loved to go after the wily river-bottom whitetails around his ranch and he wrote several classic stories about the challenges of hunting them.

In this studio photograph, our president-to-be poses for the camera wearing his favorite buckskins and holds one of his favorite rifles, an engraved Winchester Model 1876 with a half magazine in .45-75 caliber. Note the custom sterling silver Bowie knife in his belt made by Tiffany and Co. in New York.

Considered by many to be one of our greatest presidents, Theodore Roosevelt was a larger-than-life hunter, naturalist, conservationist, prolific writer and author of 42 books, statesman, rancher, war hero, adventurer, outdoorsman and recipient of the Nobel Prize. He became the nation's 26th president, the youngest in history at age 42, after the assassination of William McKinley in 1901. Among his many achievements, his work in conservation remains unprecedented. He was a driving force behind the conservation movement that started in the early 1900s. Although his life spanned only 60 short years (1858-1919), Mr. Roosevelt was a passionate, high-energy individual who packed a great deal of living into that time. The photo was taken in a New York studio, circa 1886.

⌃ THREE QUINTESSENTIAL DEER RIFLES

Could the three men in this photo be a father and two sons? Their body language suggests they might be. Even if they aren't, they've found a way to team up and fill the meat pole to capacity. With this kind of success, it's little wonder they did it with three classic deer rifles that helped tame the Eastern deer woods.

The older gentleman on the left is holding a Winchester Model 1895 lever action. The man seated has a Remington Model 8, while the man on the right has a Winchester Model 1907. Three great choices by three seasoned woodsmen. Circa 1910 to 1915.

➤ A FUTURE DEERSLAYER

Brandishing his trusty Savage Model 99, this proud father has the best of both worlds – a fine buck hanging and a son who obviously wants to follow in his father's footsteps as a slayer of mighty bucks. Dad is making sure his son gets off to a good start with a Daisy lever-action air rifle. Daisy began manufacturing lever-action BB guns like this one around 1903, and their popularity throughout the 20th century has been enormous. Many a prospective young deer hunter honed his or her shooting skills with a Daisy. In no time this determined youngster will be graduating to a .22 rifle and later on, to a full-fledged deer rifle like his dad is holding. Circa 1910.

▲ SPOILS OF THE HUNT

Nothing exemplifies the thrill of the hunt more than fresh venison in camp and the tools of the trade responsible for such positive results. Taken in Wisconsin or Minnesota, this picture of four happy hunters, probably of Scandinavian descent, dates to the early 1900s. The pipe-smoking hunter on the left is proudly showing off his Winchester Model 1895. The gun was available in several calibers, even chambered for the hard-hitting .405 Winchester cartridge introduced in 1904, and the rifle became popular with big-game hunters everywhere.

Theodore Roosevelt highly prized the Model 1895 and bought one for each of his officers during the Spanish-American War in 1898. Those rifles were chambered in .30

Army, also known as .30-40 Krag. Later, on advice from the great gunwriter Elmer Keith, President Roosevelt used a Model 1895 in .405 Winchester during his renowned African safari in 1909-10.

The man standing second from the left in the photo has a Winchester or Marlin lever-action rifle resting on his shoulder, while the man next to him is wielding a double-barrel shotgun. The pipe-smoking man on the far right is holding a Model 1893 Marlin lever action with a tang sight. Leaning in the doorway behind him is another lever-action Winchester or Marlin. It's not clear who the lucky hunter in the group might be, but there will certainly be some celebrating in camp tonight!

A MAN'S MOST CHERISHED POSSESSIONS

This turn-of-the-century whitetail mount occupies a special place in this high-ceiling, wall-papered parlor. The lower rifle cradled by upturned deer hooves is a Savage Model 99. The long gun just above the deer's head is a Marlin 1898 pump shotgun, also held with upturned deer hooves. Two late 1800s revolvers hang on the pair of steer horns while a leather "possibles" bag hangs from one of the steer horns. A hunting knife rounds out the prized assortment of hunting gear. Written at the bottom of this photo postcard is the following description: "$15.00 mount, two lower feet and rack attached, curly birch, hand craved." Photo circa 1915.

RAINY-DAY BUCKS

Having just arrived back on the main drag in town after a successful trip into the backcountry in their dependable Tin Lizzie, these two well-dressed hunters are wearing canvas rain slickers and toting classic Winchester lever-action rifles. The man on the left has a full-length rifle while his partner has a shorter saddle-ring carbine. The two bucks could easily be Texas or Oklahoma deer. The Model T Ford appears to be a 1916-era touring car. Photo circa 1916.

A GRAND SEASON IN MAINE

Postmarked April 1919, this photo postcard was sent from Rome, Maine, to a friend named Junius Cook fighting in France during World War I, c/o of the American Expeditionary Force, A.P.O. 717. The sender, Harvey S., writes: "Picture on card is yours truly with my share of 1917 deer hunt. We are looking forward to you coming to Rome." Let's hope Junius made it back from the Great War.

Harvey's share of the 1917 deer hunt was quite spectacular. His 1895 Winchester certainly performed up to its expectations in the deer woods. The Model 1895 was the first Winchester rifle to feature a box magazine instead of the tubular magazine. This allowed the rifle to safely chamber military and hunting cartridges with pointed bullets (spitzers). The '95 was used by some Americans during the Spanish American War, and about 300,000 Model 1895 rifles were sold to the Russian Empire during World War I. This was the last lever-action rifle ever designed by John Browning.

MEMORIES OF A SPECIAL DAY

With a beautifully carved oak-wood panel that includes a gun rest made from the buck's hooves, this impressive dark-antlered whitetail appears to have a normal five-point antler on its left side with four points on its right, including an exceptionally long brow tine at least 10 inches in length. Although the splayed ears and "bug" eyes could use some help, this is not a bad shoulder mount for turn-of-the-century taxidermy work.

The rifle is a classic Winchester lever action, probably Fancy Sporting Model as it has a short magazine and a sleek metal crescent buttplate. Popular Winchester lever-action deer rifles included the Models 1873, 1876, 1886, 1892, 1894, 1895, and the Model 71, 53, 55 and 64. There were many calibers, barrels, sights and other options available for each model, offering hunters a huge variety to choose from. This photo postcard is dated July 24, 1916, and postmarked Bristol, Conn.

THOSE DARING YOUNG MEN AND THE GUNS THEY CHERISHED

The photographer who set up this photo obviously knew what he was doing as the composition is picture perfect; 10 proud and happy Michigan hunters, 11 bucks and one bear on the pole, a snowshoe for effect and an amazing assortment of the most popular deer rifles of the day. The shadows behind these men indicate the photographer was using some type of high-powered lighting or flash. Sorting through the classic array of firepower the eyes of the viewer can feast upon one Winchester Model 1895, two other lever-action Winchesters, four Savage 99s, one sporterized Model 1917 Enfield and two Remington Model 14 pump-action rifles. No wonder these hunters are smiling!

ANOTHER MEMORABLE SEASON

Jim Stroud of Binghampton, N.Y., shows off his dandy buck taken near the Pennsylvania border with his accurate Model 94 Winchester saddle-ring carbine. Throughout most of the 20th century, the Model 94 Winchester lever-action rifle was arguably the most popular deer gun in the Northeast. Photo circa early 1930s.

PALMETTOS AND PINE TREES

Due to the dense vegetation of the coastal plain country of the Southeast – from Virginia all the way around to Texas – where much of the hunting was done with large packs of hounds, Southern hunters like this seasoned veteran often preferred to use double-barrel shotguns that could be streamlined for the type of hunting they did. The revolutionary new hunting rifles of the 20th century were slow to reach the South because greenback dollars were usually scarce. Out of necessity, these die-hard outdoorsmen made do with the rifles and shotguns that had been passed down from their fathers and grandfathers.

Traditionally, dog hunters loaded their guns with "buck'n ball," that is, one barrel held 00 buckshot for quick, close shots at running deer while the second barrel held a round ball for longer shots. Despite their lack of high-tech firepower, these determined hunters always brought home their fair share of game. Note the hound resting in the background. Photo taken in central Florida, circa 1920.

Courtesy Weatherby, Inc.

◄ WINCHESTER COUNTRY

It's doubtful this proud Michigan hunter took all of this game with his trusty Winchester Model 1895 lever action, but we can be sure that the fine buck pictured fell to this classic rifle. The snowshoe hares and the grouse – he no doubt used a shotgun to collect them. This was one glorious day in the Michigan woods he'll remember for the rest of his life. Photo circa 1920.

▼ PINCH ME TO MAKE SURE IT'S REAL

This proud farmer shows off his outstanding buck taken with a Winchester Model 1907. The popular semiautomatic rifle was chambered in the .351 WSL (Winchester Self-Loading) centerfire cartridge fed by a five- or 10-round box magazine. Winchester produced the enduring rifle from 1907 to 1957. Photo circa 1920.

‹ CLYDE AND HIS TRUSTY MODEL 8

‹ CLYDE AND HIS TRUSTY MODEL 8

His Remington Model 8 has spoken, and now our stalwart hunter is faced with the task of getting his deer back to camp. With a heavy winter coat, the deer is a 6-month-old doe fawn. No location is given, but on the back of the photo is written the name "Clyde." Photo circa 1920.

› A LEGENDARY G-MAN AND DEER HUNTER

Not only did he tame the deer woods with a classic rifle – a Savage Model 99 – this legendary Georgia hunter also helped tame the wild and woolly mountains of north Georgia during the golden days of bootlegging and illicit whiskey in the 1930s, '40s and '50s. A federal agent in the North Georgia Mountains for 35 years, Duff Floyd became a living legend in his own right. While chasing trippers (vehicles carrying illegal whiskey) during hundreds of high speed chases on treacherous mountain roads, he never wrecked a government vehicle, and he usually caught his man. The famed "Thunder Road," (Highway 9 in Dawson County, Ga.) became the fodder for the classic 1950s movie, *Thunder Road,* starring Robert Mitchum.

When stalking through the woods to raid a still, Duff was said to have possessed the skills of an Indian. This uncanny ability in the woods no doubt helped him track down more than a few good Georgia mountain bucks like the one pictured here. Duff retired in 1964 after a long, illustrious career. Photo circa 1949.

This confident hunter's idea of heaven on earth may well be a Winchester rifle in his hand, a pair of Maine hunting shoes on his feet and two fine bucks hanging on the buck pole. What else could a mortal deer hunter ask for? Did he take both of these outstanding bruisers with his ever-dependable lever-action Winchester? He certainly has that self-assured look on his face as he fondly caresses his Model 1892 a popular Sporting Rifle variation with a half octagon barrel and half magazine. Our hero could be somewhere in Maine as he is wearing a pair of iconic rubber-soled Maine hunting shoes sold by L.L. Bean of Freeport, Maine. Photo circa 1930.

› A MARLIN MAN

Standing next to his outstanding 9-pointer, this proud, smiling hunter is holding popular Marlin lever-action rifle with a half magazine. The popular Marlin Model 1893 was the first Marlin design made for smokeless powder cartridges, and was manufactured through 1936, at which time the classic 36, or 336 as it became known, began its long career as one of the most popular whitetail rifles of the latter half of the 20th century. Photo circa 1925.

A TIME TO REFLECT

Wearing a checkered Mackinaw so often seen in the Adirondacks and northern Maine, this proud hunter is admiring the largest of four nice bucks as he stands outside his rustic hunting cabin in the wilderness. He is holding the popular Winchester Model 1895. Could it be that the largest set of antlers on the buck pole fell to his classic rifle? Photo circa 1920.

75 YEARS OF DEER HUNTING AND ONE MORE OPENING DAY

It's opening day of the 1955 season, and 91-year-old Hiram Knox sits patiently in his chair near a deer crossing in New Hampshire. Armed with his trusty .30-30 Winchester Model 94, he's ready for action. The 1955 season marked his 75th year of chasing whitetails. He was forced to sit in a chair because he claimed that his legs were "going back" on him. "Hunters today are too excited and nervous," he added cheerfully. Mr. Knox began his deer-hunting career in 1880 when he was 16 years old. Do you think he might have been using an old '73 or '76 Winchester repeater way back when? The stories this man could tell!

A BABE IN THE WOODS

Can you guess who this proud hunter is? Although the three Canadian bucks tied to the hood of a late-model 1930s sedan are not posed in the most tasteful light for the camera, the nearest one does have a very impressive set of antlers. If you guessed the "King of Home Run Hitters" you win the jackpot. The photo was taken after a 1937 hunting trip to Nova Scotia. The Great Bambino was hunting with Outfitter Bill Lovett about 50 miles from Yarmouth. His guide was Louie A. Vacon. An article about the hunt, written by Bob Edge, later appeared in *Outdoor Life* magazine.

Babe Ruth retired from baseball in 1935. At a strapping 6 feet, 2 inches tall, he played 22 seasons in the Major League and hit 714 home runs. He tried his hand at managing, but gave it up in 1936. Although he was a true superstar and beloved national celebrity who still made numerous personal appearances in 1937, retirement gave him plenty of time to devote to deer hunting and other outdoor pursuits.

> **Deer hunting, to the dyed-in-the-wool deer hunter, is much more than a healthful sport and relaxing pastime; it is a burning obsession. When opening day rolls around, all ailing deer hunters crawl out of their sickbeds and stagger into the deer coverts, where they rapidly recover. No genuine deer hunter will allow himself to die until he has made one more hunting season, and, as there is always another hunting season coming up, it is quite obvious that all true deer hunters live forever!**

Tom Hayes
Hunting the Whitetail Deer, 1960

CHAPTER 10

AMERICA'S LOVE AFFAIR WITH WHITETAILS

American's love affair with white-tailed deer started out very slowly. Too many other life or death priorities were standing in the way. But whitetails were there every step of the journey, offering up their skins for clothing and their meat for sustenance to any and all takers. And there were many. While the early explorers were obsessed with finding gold and riches, one of the richest resources in the East from Florida to Maine stood right under the settler's noses, yet it took almost a generation to realize just how beneficial this renewable resource could be. Once the whitetail's three main attributes were recognized, food, clothing and economic wealth, it didn't take long for the new breed of Americans to exploit this amazing creature. An entire industry was established based on its flesh and skin.

Each of the 13 original colonies developed its own white-tailed deer legacy steeped in tradition; meat hunting, hide and market hunting, and later, sport hunting. Each colony had its own spirit, history, culture and distinct hunting rituals that were spawned locally.

Interestingly, today's history books still teach our youngsters that two of the most important food items found in the New World and later widely adapted were native wild turkeys and maize. While deer were feeding hungry pioneers and keeping them from starving, the importance of whitetails as a food staple seems to have been grossly ignored. The turkey was unique because it was native only to the New World, and it was quickly imported to Europe where it became a big favorite.

Certain cultivated plants introduced to the Europeans by the Eastern Indians like corn (maize), squash, pumpkins, beans, sweet potatoes and peppers were also imported across the Atlantic, where these revolutionary new food items became enormously popular. Perhaps deer were overlooked and taken for granted in the New World because there were deer in the Old World – although they were not whitetails and they were seldom hunted by the average citizens.

Most of the New World settlers came from generations of farming or skilled labor backgrounds with little to no hunting and fishing experience. It took most Europeans a considerable amount of time to adapt to a New World hunting tradition. It was a skill that did not come easy for most. Instead of recognizing the great value and potential of the native whitetails that were virtually there for the taking, most of the early settlers struggled with trying to raise Old World livestock like cattle, sheep and pigs.

In 1607, when captured by the Powhatan Indians while sailing up the Chickahominy River, Captain John Smith was fed a supper of "10 pounds of bread and a quarter of venison."

During the much-celebrated first Thanksgiving Day feast observed by the pilgrims in 1621, it was noted that the Indians who joined in the day's festivities brought with them "four or five deer." These sacrificial whitetails certainly fed more people than a couple of scrawny wild turkeys.

In chapter one of *The Eastern Trail*, edited by L. James Bashline, writer Al Shimmel notes that, "History fails to record how many volunteers in the War for Independence were sustained by the original 'combat ration,' parched corn and jerky (venison jerky)."

Once it started, America's never-ending love affair with whitetails went full steam ahead like an out-of-control freight train. Extreme exploitation saw numbers plummet to all-time lows nationwide by 1900, but thanks to prudent conservation measures, America's deer made a strong comeback in the early 20th century. So strong, in fact, that by the end of the century, game managers were pulling their hair out trying to figure out ways to better control populations. The challenges for the new century are just as complex. Yet somehow, the amazing animal that enabled so many American pioneers to survive many a bleak winter was a survivor itself.

Dr. Leonard Lee Rue III, one of the great whitetail photographers of the 20th century, said it best in his celebrated 1962 book, *The World of the White-tailed Deer:* "It has often been said that the last living creature to survive on this earth will probably be an insect. However, the white-tailed deer, which has outlived such early predators as the saber-toothed tiger, disease, starvation, hunting and mismanagement, seems a likely possibility as a chief competitor for the last remaining herbage on earth."

◄ CAPTURING A KODAK MOMENT

A century ago, few – if any – of the deer camp photographers who picked up a camera by chance and recorded the events of the day on film ever gave a second thought as to the importance of what their timeless photographic gems would mean to the future. They simply wanted to capture the moment. But if it hadn't been for these unsung heroes, like this kindred spirit, who grabbed a camera instead of a rifle and took time to compose the countless deer camp photos that we treasure so much today, modern-day hunting enthusiasts would have missed out on a very special piece of history. We owe these men an immense debt. Thanks to them, we're able to travel back in time 100 years or more and get a unique, firsthand glimpse into the golden days of yesteryear. Photo circa 1920s.

◄ OLD WAYS DIE HARD

Two rugged men, possibly father and son, pose with their Civil War-era muskets, now being used to hunt four-legged critters instead of the two-legged variety. Since the head and antlers resting atop the huge ox appear to be the severed head only, do you suppose they plan to mount their 8-point trophy and hang it on the wall? Despite the wide array of innovative new rifles available for deer hunting after the Civil War, some hunters continued to use single-shot muskets and muzzleloaders that had been converted from flintlocks to percussion rifles and passed down through the family. This was particularly true in economically depressed areas. Photo circa 1870s.

▲ A SERIOUS WHITETAIL HUNTER

Could this seasoned deerslayer be one of America's original whitetail fanatics? Unlike today, having all of your trophies mounted by a competent taxidermist and displayed on a wall for a photograph was almost unheard of a century ago. When a man went to the trouble of having his trophy collection mounted and photographed for posterity, you know he was serious about his sport.

The deer-hoof coat rack and the mounted heads on the ornamental backboards certainly indicate that this seasoned hunter revered and respected his quarry. Likely having endured its share of cold and snowy winters, the log cabin is reminiscent of a prairie scene. The well-used Winchester '95 this hunter is holding could certainly tell some tales. Photo circa early 1900s.

▼ THE THRILL OF A LIFETIME

Since the dawn of deer hunting in America, this stirring scene has been repeated over and over again wherever whitetails are found. A hunter makes what he thinks is a good shot, and the quarry runs off. Doubt, that much despised enemy of all serious hunters, begins to seep in. Was it a good shot after all? Time begins to move in slow motion as the sportsman breathlessly follows a scant blood trail through heavy brush. Where will the trail lead?

Suddenly, the hunter looks ahead, and in a heart-pounding rush of relief, gratitude and gut-wrenching emotion, all doubt disappears. The buck of a lifetime lies in the path ahead, waiting to be recovered. What a buck it is, let the campfire tales begin! From an unmarked stereoview, circa 1907.

547. "That Last Shot Fixed Him."

▶ MAKING HISTORY IN OHIO

For the first time since the early 1880s when the deer season was permanently closed due to dwindling deer numbers, Ohio opened a legal deer hunting season over a three-county area in December 1943. The hunt took place in the sprawling Roosevelt-Shawnee Game Preserve. It was reported that hunters flocked to the area in such large numbers that at least 250 hopeful deerslayers had to be turned away.

Since wartime rationing of meat was a fact of life in 1943, many of the hunters who participated were hoping to collect a few pounds of venison for the table. One of the more fortunate hunters was Paul Ralston, of Dayton. He, accompanied by his wife, not only collected some tasty venison with his classic Browning Auto-5 shotgun, but he also ended the day by shooting the buck of a lifetime, an outstanding 10-point trophy weighing in at 180 pounds.

‹ CALL OF THE WILD

CALL OF THE WILD

These two gentlemen have come home with a fine bag, each with a buck and doe. The hunter on the left, sporting a finely checkered Savage Model 99, also has taken a fine young black bear. His partner, holding a Remington Model 14 or Model 141, displays a snowshoe hare. It's a good bet these two veteran outdoorsmen have been trekking the wild together for many seasons. Photo circa 1935.

⋀ A MEMORABLE HUNT IN THE CATSKILLS

These three bucks were taken in the famous Catskill Mountains of southern New York where deer hunters and trout fishermen have been plying their trade since the mid-1800s. Famed outdoor writer and gunsmith Larry Koller endeared Sullivan County to thousands of sportsmen around the country in his classic 1948 book, *Shots at Whitetails*.

The tall young man on the left grasping the antler of the largest buck is holding a heavy double-barrel shotgun. Second from left, the young man wearing a World War I Army campaign hat is armed with a Winchester Model 1907 semiautomatic rifle equipped with a 10-round box magazine. The Model 1907 utilized a .351 WSL cartridge, and when fired from a rifle carried the energy better than that of a modern .357 Magnum cartridge. The handy '07 remained in production from 1907 to 1957.

The young man wearing the tie and sweater is holding a .30-40 Krag-Jorgensen with a sporterized stock, very popular with deer and big-game hunters across the nation in the early 20th century. Not to be outdone, the older gentleman on the right has a long-barrel Winchester lever action. From a photo postcard circa 1920.

➤ LIVING OFF THE LAND

The idea of living off the land was not as far-fetched in the early 20th century as it might be today. Wild places where a man could get lost and find plenty of game still existed in many areas, and some men answered that call. This rugged individual, clutching his trustworthy Winchester that is never far away, looks as if he might have just taken off his snowshoes after a morning's sojourn of checking his trapline in the newly fallen snow. On his way home, he waylaid a sleek doe for table fare. Now it's time to sit a spell and relax. His catch is impressive; a number of prime fox pelts, several raccoons, striped skunks and muskrat skins. A second Winchester leans against the wall. Photo circa mid-1920s.

◄ LEGENDARY FOREST RANGER ARTHUR WOODY POSES WITH A BOW

During the inaugural and highly publicized five-day archery hunt in the Blue Ridge Wildlife Management Area in the North Georgia Mountains in 1940, District Forest Ranger Arthur Woody mockingly poses with a primitive "bow and arrer." Ranger Woody began stocking deer in the area 13 years earlier in 1927. He had initially hand-raised five fawns and released them into the refuge when they were about 1 year old. Thirteen years later, after stocking several dozen more deer, the herd had grown to an estimated 2,000 animals.

The archery hunt was the first modern hunt of its kind in the nation. The Blue Ridge WMA was also the first wildlife management area ever established in the nation, being Ranger Woody's brainchild. Knowing how difficult it would be to shoot one of these mountain deer with a bow and arrow, he predicted that no one would kill a deer with a bow, and challenged the 30 or so hunters who participated by telling them he would "eat the snout of any deer brought into camp." His prediction proved correct. No deer were accounted for on that first hunt.

PURE ELATION

Any day spent in the deer woods makes a man glad to be alive, and these two hunters obviously have had a fine morning's adventure in the wilds of Florida. The younger man on the right wearing leather snake leggings holds both shotguns, as the older gentleman on the left proudly cradles the results of the day's hunt. Were these men dog hunting with a larger group? It's difficult to say, but one thing is clear: The joy expressed in their faces comes from their passion for hunting America's most beloved big-game animal. Photo circa 1940.

NO MORE MEAT RATIONING HERE

While his son is probably off fighting in the war somewhere, this stalwart Pennsylvania patriot has done his part in the war effort by providing fresh meat for the rest of the family. Two fine yearling bucks lay across the hood of his weathered 1938 Dodge sedan.

During the later decades of the 20th century, Pennsylvania was known for having the highest number of licensed deer hunters in the nation. More than a million hunters took to the woods each year, and schools often closed on opening day to accommodate the family tradition of going deer hunting. Although no one liked to talk about it, it was a well-known fact that over 90 percent of the annual harvest consisted of yearling bucks. Today, thanks to much improved management, that number has changed drastically. More young bucks are reaching maturity than ever before.

But going back to yesteryear, the situation was much the same. Even in 1942 when this photo was taken, the majority of bucks shot were yearlings. While Pennsylvania may forever have to live with that stigma, one thing is certain: no finer eating exists in the world than a tender young deer.

TOUGHING OUT
ANOTHER COLD WINTER

These hungry whitetails are yarded up in deep snow near Farragut, Idaho, taking advantage of the feed provided by the game department. Note the absence of bucks in the photo. They are probably deeper in the woods, hiding from the workers and the photographer. Photo circa 1930.

HISTORY IN THE MAKING

North Carolina Forest Ranger Lester Schaap checks in a fine mountain buck at the famous Cantrell Creek Wilderness Hunt Camp in the Pisgah Game Reserve during the third annual wilderness hunt in the fall of 1938. The hunting camp was located in Turkey Pen Gap in the heart of the Pisgah National Forest. Since deer and bears had been protected in western North Carolina in the late 1800s and early 1900s by wealthy landowners like the Vanderbilt family who had accumulated vast land holdings, big-game populations were never wiped out as they were in other parts of the southern Appalachians. In the North Georgia Mountains, for instance, hungry pioneers and settlers had hunted deer and bears down to the last animal with large packs of dogs and fire torches at night. By 1900, both species had all but disappeared from that region.

Managed deer hunts at Cantrell Creek Wilderness Hunt Camp began in 1936. This popular hunt in western North Carolina was enjoyed by hundreds of sportsmen in the late 1930s. The camp in Turkey Pen Gap could be reached only after a five-mile hike. All provisions and equipment had to be packed in by hunters, but the U.S. Forest Service provided tents, cots and firewood. Groups of 25 sportsmen hunted the primitive area for an entire week. Bag limits included one deer or bear per hunter. Photo by renowned U.S. Forest Service photographer Clint Davis, 1938.

A BLOSSOMING BOWHUNTER

Bowhunting garnered considerable media attention during the 1930s, '40s and '50s, and hunters who took up the challenge were often referred to as "modern-day Robin Hoods." Using a longbow and wooden arrows tipped with Bear broadheads, Bob Brewer of Indianapolis proudly stands next to a hefty Indiana forkhorn that he managed to bring down on his very first archery hunt. Several years of dedicated practice really paid off on opening day in Brown County in November 1959. Brewer was only in the woods for a few hours when the buck showed up. The arrow protruding from the deer's back was probably placed there for the photo to show where it had penetrated the buck's vitals on its right side. Associated Press Wire photo, 1959.

A GEORGIA ODDITY

What's all the hoopla? Why is this group of Georgia farmers gathered around this medium-size buck? In the late 1930s, there were no deer in South Georgia to speak of because they had all been wiped out during the previous century. Every once in a while, however, a random buck would show up from parts unknown, and some lucky soul like the young farmhand pictured with the double-barrel shotgun would collect a rare trophy. Whenever this happened, it was front page news! Georgia's highly successful deer restoration program throughout the central and southern portion of the state would not begin for another 20 years, in the mid-1950s.

SEMPER FI!

Among his many timely quotes, President Ronald Reagan made the following statement in 1985, "Some people spend an entire lifetime wondering if they made a difference in the world. But, Marines don't have that problem."

Even though these innovative Marines might have missed opening day back home in the states, they more than made up for it in the frigid no-man's land in Korea. They may have been far from home fighting in yet another difficult war in the early 1950s, but they certainly enjoyed some home-style venison that night. These three hearty Marines were returning from a helicopter patrol along the Korean front in search of Red Guerrillas in March 1952 when they came across a pair of indigenous roe deer in the frozen wasteland. No one had to tell them what to do.

(Left to right) Edward Ponselle of White Bear Lake, Minn., Captain Arthur Rawling of Long Beach, Calif., and Major E. Kirby Smith of Helena, Tenn., proudly kneel over their bounty that will soon be simmering in the mess hall. God bless America and Semper Fi!

HEADED FOR THE BARN

Holding a well-used single-barrel shotgun, this smiling Massachusetts deerslayer can't wait to get his prize doe hung up in the barn for the skinning and butchering chore. He knows the beautiful doe on the hood of his 1940 Ford Coupe will soon be converted into many pounds of mouth-watering venison for the family to enjoy in the weeks ahead. Photo 1940.

A SPECIAL CHRISTMAS PRESENT

Christmas dinner on Dec. 25, 1939, at the home of Mr. and Mrs. Jack Duggan of Whinnery's Resort at Au Sable Lake in Ogemaw County, Mich., was interrupted when Jack happened to look out the window and spot a doe that had fallen on the slick ice about 500 feet from shore while trying to cross the partially frozen lake. With all four legs sprawled out on the thin ice, the doe was unable to get up.

Since the ice was dangerously thin, the couple and their son Jack got into a boat and inched their way toward the struggling animal. Using great caution because of the doe's flailing hooves, Jack was able to get his belt around the deer's neck and pull her safely into the boat. Once back at shore, the doe was unable to walk. The Duggans massaged the doe's muscles and walked her around for a bit. After several minutes, the fortunate animal seemed to regain her composure and bounded off into the woods. The Duggans

resumed their dinner festivities feeling gratified and up-lifted about their part in the rescue effort.

The accompanying newspaper caption read:

"Mr. and Mrs. Jack Duggan and William Duggan, of Au Sable Lake in Ogemaw County, had a cold Christmas dinner but a warm glow in their hearts on Christmas day because they had saved a life. To be sure the life they saved was only that of a doe deer but the Duggans thought it was important enough to risk their own in the successful rescue attempt. The animal had fallen about 500 feet off shore while cross-ing the lake and was unable to get back on its feet because of a glass-like sheet of ice. In the above photo, Jack Duggan is shown as he neared the trapped animal to pull it into his boat. The rescuers had to use the boat because the ice was not strong enough to support their weight."

POSING FOR A PICTURE

This man certainly isn't dressed for hunting. In fact, he might have just stepped off his Harley, but he doesn't seem to mind posing for the camera with such a regal 8-point buck in front of the local grocery store. Several people are also checking out this scene and standing next to the photographer, as evidenced by the shadows on the porch. The hunter who shot the deer likely is enjoying the attention. Photo circa 1930.

A SPECIAL HUNT
IN MORE WAYS THAN ONE

Father and son stand next to two large does riding atop their 1942 Chevrolet Fleetwood after spending what must have been a memorable day in the woods together. The vehicle license is a mid-1940s tag from Pennsylvania.

Since the war was raging at this time, it could be that the young man pictured was home on leave for an all-too-short time, and was lucky enough to spend a singular day of deer hunting with his dad.

LOADED DOWN
WITH TROPHY BUCKS

It's not often that you see this many outstanding bucks heaped together on the hood of one vehicle. The Dodge truck dates to the early 1940s as very little cosmetic change occurred in these trucks from 1939 to about 1947. The location is unknown, but judging from the fact that the three bucks are not overly large in body size, and the fact that the man in the foreground has his sleeves rolled up, the weather appears to be fairly mild, indicating the photo could have been taken in the southern portion of the U.S. It's a good thing this hunter has his sleeves rolled up... He has his work cut out for him!

HOME FROM ANOTHER GREAT HUNT

Dated November 1947, longtime hunting companions John and Vern untie their sleek 4-point buck from the front fender of a 1946 Dodge as Bozo the pit bull hungrily looks on. No location is given for this snowy scene, but if you use your imagination, it could be just about anywhere in the U.S. where snow piles deep come November in the deer woods.

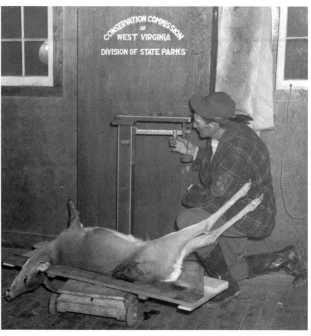

WEIGHING IN

A hunter weighs his doe after a successful hunt on public land in West Virginia in 1946. Hunters were required to bring any deer killed to the checking station and have a tag affixed showing the hunter's name, the location of the kill and the weight of the deer. With a good luck feather in his hat and wearing a shoulder patch that says "West Virginia Game Protector," this hunter knows he will enjoy many pounds of scrumptious venison in the weeks ahead.

A PROUD MOMENT FOR THE SNAGGY ROD & GUN CLUB

These five members of the Snaggy Rod & Gun Club on Maryland's Eastern Shore, successful and prominent businessmen all, proudly show off the results of an unforgettable 1955 hunt. With rifles in hand they are left to right: Melvin R. Kenny Jr. (a Republican Delegate to 3rd District in Baltimore), William Frank Downey Jr. (president of the club), Richard P. Moser, Herbert H. Tyler and Nick Nestor. Photo by Dorsey Studios, Baltimore, Md.

INTERVIEW AT ROCK CREEK REFUGE

A WSB Radio reporter from Atlanta interviews two successful hunters during a special firearms hunt at the rugged Blue Ridge Wildlife Management Area in the North Georgia Mountains in November 1941 (known locally as Rock Creek Refuge). A local game warden stands on the left as legendary Ranger Arthur Woody observes the interview from the right. The hunter on the left is holding a Winchester lever action while his partner is armed with a sporterized 1917 Enfield .30-06. This was the second season the 40,000-acre wilderness refuge had been opened up to a controlled

hunt conducted jointly by the state of Georgia and the U.S. Forest Service. Both archery and firearms hunts were held.

In 1927, Ranger Woody, who eventually managed over 200,000 acres of national forestland as a District Ranger with the Forest Service, had begun stocking the refuge with deer purchased from North Carolina with his own money. Within 13 short years, his well-protected herd grew from a few animals to several thousand. During the early 1940s, Ranger Woody, who later became known fondly as the

"Barefoot Ranger of Suches," became one of the most famous and high-profile forest rangers in the nation due to his many innovative and visionary conservation practices.

The managed hunts at Blue Ridge WMA became media events that received considerable national and local news coverage. Ironically, only a few weeks after this photo was taken, the Japanese bombed Pearl Harbor on Dec. 7, forever changing the United States and the world.

OPENING DAY MAGIC

The quest for a buck can be a very personal thing as evidenced by what this hunter's wife wrote on the back of his photograph.

"Nov. 1953
"That's Benny (the dog) with Guy. He got the deer at 8 a.m., opening day. It was such a warm sunny day. We could scarcely believe it when he came home so soon – Brian sure thought his dad was great!"

OLD FLINTLOCK

Famed 20th century South Carolina deer hunter and writer Archibald Rutledge (1883-1973), nicknamed Old Flintlock, immortalized the thrill of hunting whitetails with hounds in and around his beloved Hampton Plantation just north of Charleston. Throughout his long lifetime, Rutledge wrote dozens of stories and a number of books devoted to his passion. A naturalist, poet and true lover of wildlife, no one captured the essence of hunting deer with hounds better than he did. Listening to their sweet music was part of his being.

The buck came down to the water's edge, and when he got to about 50 yards I stood up and threw the gun up to my face. He kept coming and I let him come. At about 25 yards he suddenly saw me, snorted, and leaped to his left as if somebody had unsnapped a spring in him. I forgot he was a deer. I shot at him as you'd lead a duck or a quail on a quartering shot, plenty of lead ahead of his shoulder.

"I pulled the trigger – for some odd reason shooting the choke barrel – right in the middle of a spring that had him six feet off the ground and must have been wound up to send him 20 yards, into the bush and out of my life. The gun said boom! But I didn't hear it. The gun kicked but I didn't feel it. All I saw was that this monster came down out of the sky like I'd shot me an airplane. He came down flat, turning completely over and landing on his back, and he never wiggled.

"The dogs came up ferociously and started to grab him, but they had sense and knew he didn't need any extra grabbing. I'd grabbed him real good, with about three ounces of No. 1 buckshot in the choke barrel. I had busted his shoulder and busted his neck and dead-centered his heart. I had let him get so close that you could practically pick the wads out of his shoulder. This was my buck. Nobody else had shot him. Nobody else had seen him but me. Nobody had advised or helped. This monster was mine.

Robert Ruark
The Old Man and the Boy, 1957

CHAPTER 11

THE SWEETEST MUSIC I EVER HEARD

Legendary whitetail author Archibald Rutledge (1883-1973) grew up in South Carolina and hunted to the music of the hounds in and around his beloved plantation near Charleston for some eight decades. During his long and productive lifetime, he wrote over 50 books and hundreds of magazine stories. Much of his writing was focused on his favorite subject – nature and whitetail hunting. He served as poet laureate in South Carolina from 1934 to 1973, and many of his classic poems revolved around deer hunting. His stories often appeared in *Outdoor Life* and *Field & Stream*. Among his most revered hunting books were *Old Plantation Days* (1907), *Plantation Game Trails* (1921), *An American Hunter* (1937) and *Those Were the Days* (1955).

Rutledge's stories written during the first half of the 20th century immortalized the magic of hunting deer with well-trained hounds, a tradition that originated during colonial days. Today, this deeply rooted American ritual is generally considered a Southern tradition, since the legal use of dogs for whitetail hunting has in modern times been restricted to coastal areas of the Deep South only.

But, there was a time in our past when hounds were used by hunters up and down the East Coast from Florida to New England, in Ontario and eastern Canada and across the interior of the U.S. wherever wily whitetails were pursued. By the early 1800s, this all-too-efficient means of collecting venison had been outlawed in most places. Although still legal in eight southern states – in coastal plain regions from Virginia to Louisiana – the centuries old tradition is disappearing at a rapid rate. Chances are it will become extinct altogether in the not so distant future.

This sad truth is due in part to the fact that land ownership patterns have changed drastically during the past 100 years. Whereas a man at one time could turn his dogs out on thousands upon thousands of acres of land without ever crossing a property line, today many of the large tracts of yesteryear have been divided and reduced into much smaller parcels – in many cases 100 acres or less – not conducive to hunting with packs of dogs.

For those lucky souls who have experienced the heart-thumping excitement of sitting in the woods and listening to the music of Walkers and redbones, black and tans and every cross in between, the thrill of hearing those yapping dogs getting closer and closer and suddenly having a buck jump out of the brush and bound out in front of you will, for many, always represent the heart and soul of the deer hunting scene.

5089. In Camp among the Pines.

▲ A WELL-DESERVED RESPITE

With an innovative shelter fashioned out of white pine saplings and boughs, it's easy to see why this old stereoview is titled "In Camp among the Pines." Dated 1889, the picture depicts two pipe-smoking hunters reflecting on their good fortune while several brown and white Walker hounds take a break after a fruitful morning's chase. The hunter in the foreground is leaning on his well-used double-barrel muzzleloader while a large, mature doe hangs next to him. Photographed and published by B.W. Kilburn of Littleton, N.H.

4972. Monarch of the Hills.

▲ MONARCH OF THE HILLS

The morning's chase has been an exciting one, and these happy hunters are only too glad to take turns carrying this large buck back to camp on a pole. The hound on the left indicates the use of dogs during the hunt. From a stereoview titled "Monarch of the Hills," by B.W. Kilburn, Littleton, N.H., 1888.

Popular Series (left margin, decorative)

Popular Series (right margin, decorative)

DEER HUNTERS' CAMP IN FLORIDA.

▲ AN AFTERNOON LULL DURING THE HUNT

With a small arsenal of rabbit-eared shotguns resting against the tree trunks and the fruits of their labor hanging proudly in the same palm trees, these intrepid hunters take a midafternoon break after a successful morning of listening to the music of the dogs. Titled "Deer Hunters' Camp in Florida," this vintage stereoview comes from the late 1870s or 1880s.

Known locally as "Crackers," the rugged pioneers of central Florida struggled to eke out a living growing a few crops, establishing orange and grapefruit orchards, hunting, fishing and trapping, and in general, living off the land. In a climate where men commonly worked from sunup to sundown every day, an occasional deer hunt was a much cherished form of recreation. It also provided savory venison. But because of the nearly impenetrable cover, not to mention snakes, alligators and a host of other varmints, virtually all of the hunting was done with packs of hounds. There's even one dog curled up under a tree near the center of the photo.

Several of these men could well be Civil War veterans. The stereoview is stamped "Popular Series," known to be a pirate producer of low-quality stereoviews from the 1870s to the 1890s.

◄ THE BUCKSHOT BOYS

Although no location is given, this scene easily could have been photographed in the hills of Kentucky or Tennessee. Judging by their looks, you wouldn't want to get on the bad side of these rugged mountaineers. Could that be Pa on the right and his three sons on the left? When they're not chasing deer with the hounds, this rough-and-tumble bunch is probably tending to their still somewhere back in a mountain holler.

The dogs have earned their supper today – one nice buck and the fresh skin from a second deer. Note the powder horn carried by the young man on the left. Collectively, the "buck'n ball" that has poured out of the muzzles of the four antique shotguns held by these hunters has no doubt accounted for a passel of furry critters over the years. Photo circa 1890.

4969. Glory enough for one day.

▲ GLORY ENOUGH FOR ONE DAY

The hounds have done what they were born to do, and seven seasoned hunters and a young boy take a few moments to reflect on the day's bounty. Most of the men are wielding double-barrel shotguns, several of which are old percussion muzzleloaders. In addition to the two deer in the foreground, the man in the center of the photo is holding several fox skins. From a stereoview titled "Glory enough for one day," by B.W. Kilburn, Littleton, N.H., 1888.

➤ HUNTIN' PARTNERS

In a Southern forest where huge virgin pine and hardwood trees have recently been cut, a hunter and his pack of Walker foxhounds carry out a ritual that is as old as America itself. The side-by-side shotgun he is holding presents an enigma; it clearly has a ramrod, indicating that it is a 19th century percussion muzzleloader, yet our hero has a belt full of newfangled paper shotgun shells around his waist. One fact is certain – with a happy and raring-to-go puppy in his lap that will need plenty of training, this veteran of many a chase is once again living the dream. Photo circa early 1900s.

⋎ A BUSY CAMP SCENE FROM YESTERYEAR

Deer hunting with packs of hounds was a highly effective method of hunting brought to America by early settlers. Until laws were passed in the late 1800s banning the use of dogs in northern states because it was so effective, dog hunting was widespread in the Northeast, the Midwest and Canada. Later, after laws were passed, the tradition of using dogs remained a much revered method of hunting deer in the Southeast throughout the 20th century. Today dog hunting is still legal in portions of eight southern states, mostly in dense coastal plain areas.

With a primitive, shake-roofed cabin surrounded by several wall tents, this rustic Northern camp scene spurs the imagination. Even though one buck and the front half of a smaller

deer are hanging on the makeshift meat pole, the hounds are raring to get off their chains and once again prove their worth. On the right is a traditional Adirondack basket used for packing meat and other gear, while the lever-action rifle in the center of the photo looks like an 1873 Winchester. The photo was taken in the Northeast, circa 1880.

➤ DOG DAYS IN QUEBEC

These Walker and black and tan hounds have earned a well-deserved rest after a day of chasing several big-antlered monarchs in the wilds of eastern Quebec, Canada. One of the bucks hanging is a real brute that no doubt gave these hounds a run for their money. The caption on this photo postcard reads: "Canadian Hunting Scene, The Day's Sport (Deer)." Photo circa 1910.

HOUNDING IN ONTARIO

Before dog hunting was banned in Ontario in the late 1800s, hunting with hounds was a popular and highly efficient way of procuring lots of venison. Typical of the era, these successful hunters are wielding a variety of classic deer rifles including several Winchesters and Savage 99s. Photos circa 1895.

9447, When the old men feel young again.

Copyright 1894, by B. W. Kilburn.

⌃ HE WAS HOW BIG?!

When seasoned deer hunters get together, oh how the tall tales fly! Among a plethora of rabbit-eared shotguns and one Winchester lever action, these old veterans are surely reliving some memorable moments. Titled "When the old men feel young again," this stereoview taken by B.W. Kilburn was published in 1894. The photo was taken somewhere in New England a year or so before that. The happy black-and-tan hound and his companion played a vital role in the chase for this long-tined ol' ridge runner.

⌃ NOTHING LIKE A WARM FIRE

The day's hunt is over and the men can now sit around a roaring fire and reflect while they try to keep the chill of night at bay. What a day it has been listening to the music of the hounds. The boy seems happy to be in charge of the dog sitting next to him. No location is given but the photo may well have been taken somewhere in the Northeast shortly before hunting with packs of dogs was outlawed. Photo circa late 1800s.

◄ GETTIN' MEAT

Dated Jan. 9, 1934, these four shot-gun hunters stand next to a fine 8-point buck. The buck's small body size suggests a southern deer, and the shotguns suggest these men are members of a dog hunting club somewhere in the Deep South.

▲ THE GOOD-OL'-BOYS HAVE DONE IT AGAIN

Groups of this size were not at all unusual during the golden days of dog hunting in the Carolinas in the 1930s, '40s, '50s and '60s when large tracts of land were still available to hunt. Since some of these hunters are wearing license buttons, this photo was taken after a Saturday morning hunt in eastern North Carolina. Note that all of the firearms shown are shotguns, as buckshot is one of the most effective ways of taking running deer at short range – often the norm while hunting with hounds. Photo circa 1935.

Savage Model 99 lever-action—made in following calibers: .22 hi-power; .250-3000; .30-30; .303; and .300. Also made in special carbine style in .30-30 and .303 calibers.
Savage Model 20 bolt-action made in .250-3000 and .300 calibers.

Six straight shots—
when you need them most

One tense moment as you catch sight of your game —

Then up with your Savage—holds steady as a rock against your shoulder—points in the twinkling of an eye.

Bang goes your first shot—then if you need them, five more shots less than three seconds apart.

For the swift powerful Savage lever is ready to pump up cartridge after cartridge from the magazine with never a jam.

And in that rotary magazine you can pack your soft-nose bullets without denting the points, for each cartridge is supported *at the base*—recoil can't damage them.

There is a Savage team, rifle and cartridge, for every kind of American game. No matter what style of rifle you like, or what caliber you need, somewhere in the Savage line you will find what you are looking for.

Ask your dealer to show you the Savage or write us for a complete illustrated booklet.

SAVAGE ARMS CORPORATION
Dept. 35, Utica, N. Y.

SAVAGE = STEVENS

The Savage Sporter — Bolt action repeating rifle, round blued barrel, genuine American walnut stock, varnish finish, pistol grip, interchangeable magazine. Ideal for all kinds of small and medium game.

Model 23 A	.22 cal.	$19.50
Model 23 B	.25-20 cal.	23.50
Model 23 C	.32-20 cal.	23.50

WINCHESTERS RULE

A seasoned cowboy with an almost haughty expression on his face poses for the camera as three hunters show off the bounty of the hunt, a small-bodied West Texas whitetail buck. All three hunters are holding popular Model 94 Winchesters, probably .30-30s. A buckboard buggy appears in the background. Perhaps this proud cowboy served as a guide for the three "tenderfoot" city slickers. Photo circa late 1890s.

> **Papa had taught me that way back when I was little, the same as he'd taught me to hunt downwind from my game. He always said: 'It's not your shape that catches a deer's eye. It's your moving. If a deer can't smell you and can't see you move, he won't ever know you're there.'**

Fred Gipson
Old Yeller, 1956

CHAPTER 12

LONE STAR MEMORIES

When it comes to whitetail hunting, the Lone Star state is an enigma. Texas is a different world. The largest of the lower 48 states – only Alaska is larger in land area, Texas has long boasted the highest whitetail population and the highest deer harvest of any state in the nation. Unlike other parts of the country where you find either large-bodied deer with huge racks or small-bodied deer with smaller racks, Texas historically has produced small-bodied deer with enormous antlers.

A first-time visitor to the famed South Texas brush country might look out across the vast landscape and ask: "Where is all the wildlife?" That same visitor might note the lack of trees and water. Everything he touches will contain stickers. If he happens to crawl on the ground to stalk a deer, he might get a knee full of cactus needles for his efforts.

Upon closer inspection, though, an amazing transformation will take place. The brush country begins to come alive. Our visitor will see javelinas and wild hogs. He'll see quail by the hundreds. He'll see hawks and birds of all descriptions. He'll see bobcats and even an occasional mountain lion. If it happens to be during the rutting season, he'll see large-antlered bucks chasing does everywhere he looks. Suddenly he realizes this seemingly "barren" land is a game paradise.

Texas certainly has produced its share of dis-

tinguished trophy bucks over the years. One in particular was a former world record and one of the highest scoring whitetails of all time. The Benson Buck from Brady, Texas, reportedly killed by a cowboy in the early 1890s, boasted 78 points and later scored 286 nontypical Boone and Crockett points (see chapter 15 for more on this deer). That rich tradition of producing trophy antlers since the 1890s has continued into the 21st century.

From the early 1900s to the late 1930s, most Texans were meat hunters. In the 1930s and '40s, and particularly after World War II, more and more hunters began to eye Texas as a place where large-antlered bucks could be hunted. The new concept of leasing land to groups of hunters became very attractive to ranchers who were always looking for ways to generate income. Hunters from the cities began flocking to the hinterlands and pitching tents, hoping to meet up with a wide-antlered "Muy Grande." Out-of-state hunters began leasing hunting rights. Many of those hunters returned home without being disappointed. That rich tradition has flourished for the past 60 or 70 years.

In the late 1960s and early '70s, two hardworking Texas biologists – Al Brothers and Murphy E. Ray Jr. – began developing the fanciful concept of managing deer herds just as you might manage a cattle herd, taking into consideration all aspects of the subject: the carrying capacity of the land, antler growth, total deer harvest, predator control, diseases, nutrition and a host of other key topics. In 1975, they co-authored the now classic book, *Producing Quality Whitetails*. The modern era of white-tailed deer management had begun. Today, thanks to two visionary Texans, countless hunters across America have greatly benefited from the sound prin-ciples of quality deer management. Deer herds have become healthier and more balanced.

Next time you get a hankering to pick up a rifle and chase a gnarly ol' rutting giant, grab yourself some rattling horns and head down to toward the Rio Grande Valley. It'll be a deer hunt you'll never forget.

⌃ MUY GRANDES!

The famed brush country of South Texas has been turning out "muy grande" racks for well over 100 years, and these bruiser bucks taken in 1907 are no exception. Looks like this trio of hunters from the big city, with two rifles in scabbards and a shotgun, have certainly gotten their money's worth. The shotgun stacked with the two Winchesters was probably used for a little bird hunting on the side, as the quail hunting in turn-of-the-century South Texas was, and still is, exceptional. From a printed postcard titled, "Hunting Scene, Uvalde, Texas," dated December 1907.

A MEXICAN LION

The Mexican hunter on the left looks plenty happy that his trusty lever action put an end to a potential marauder. Believe it or not, mountain lions often prefer to prey on mature bucks instead of does or younger bucks with smaller racks. Part of the reason for this is that mature bucks are loners in rough country where mountain lions inhabit, whereas most does live in small to large groups for safety. Plus, bucks are often in rough shape after a long rutting season and more vulnerable to the large predators. The problem is not uncommon in South Texas, even in today's world of high fence and trophy management. The man on the right poses with a heavy-horned brush country buck. The photo was taken just across the Rio Grande in Mexico, although, just like today, plenty of lions made their homes in Texas around the turn of the century. Photo postcard circa 1900.

A TEXAS WALLHANGER FOR THE AGES

The classic "Cheshire cat" grin on this proud hunter's face says it all as he sits atop his 1924 Buick Coupe showing off two fine Texas bucks. The buck lying across the hood is a nice young 10-pointer that will provide plenty of delicious venison. But the huge-antlered Lone Star muy grande on the running board is the buck of a lifetime!

Truly, this deer has it all. With a main-frame 5-by-5 rack and split brow tines, a split G-2 on the right, a split G-2 and G-3 on the left, several burr points, and a long, 9-inch drop time on the right side, he'll certainly take your breath away. At least 16 points are visible in the photo, but it could have more. In today's world, this is what every hunter in Texas hopes to bring home. This awesome South Texas buck would easily gross in the high 180s or 190s as a nontypical.

Although this photo was taken nearly a century ago, somewhere in time – perhaps on a lone sendero deep in the Texas brush country – the spirit of this ecstatic hunter lives on through generations of new hunters ready to experience the thrill of a true Texas "Muy Grande."

BRUSH COUNTRY BRUISER

Posed with his heavy horned 8-pointer and his always accurate Remington Model 8, Mr. A.H. Malott of McAllen, Texas, knows he has done a good day's work. He shot the massive deer about 12 miles north of McAllen, in the heart of the South Texas brush country. Photo circa 1920s.

"A DEER HUNT, LOWER RIO GRANDE VALLEY"

This photo postcard is postmarked Harlingen, Texas, April 6, 1923. Two of the men pictured are holding Winchester carbines. The man second from the left is holding a Winchester rifle with an octagon barrel. The second man from the right appears to be wearing lace-up military boots typical of World War I and is holding a Springfield Armory Model 1903 bolt action. His belt is loaded up and ready with .30-06 rounds.

Harlingen is located in Cameron County in the heart of the Rio Grande Valley in South Texas, about 30 miles from the coast of the Gulf of Mexico, just north of McAllen and Brownsville. Some true Texas giants have come from this area during the past 100 years. In light of the fact that most large landowners and ranchers today manage their property for mature bucks, that trend has continued right up to the present time.

THREE BUCKS AND A COYOTE

From a photo postcard titled "Game found near Dalhart, Tex.," these two hunters have accounted for three nice West Texas bucks and a wily coyote with their sure-shooting Winchester Model 1907 autoloaders. The '07s came with either a five or 10-shot detachable magazine. The only cartridge offered with the rifle at that time was the .351 Winchester Self-Loading centerfire. Dalhart is northwest of Amarillo and not far from the New Mexico border. Dated 1907.

THE VICE PRESIDENT-ELECT GETS HIS BUCK

Shortly after daybreak on Nov. 16, 1932, opening day of the Texas deer season, John Garner of Uvalde, Texas, downed this hefty 8-pointer after making a 200-yard shot with his trusty Remington Model 8. Known among his contemporaries as "Cactus Jack," John Nance Garner IV (1868 - 1967) was elected the 32nd Vice President of the United States under Franklin Delano Roosevelt in 1932.

Garner served as a state representative from 1898 to 1902, and as a U.S. Congressman from 1903 to 1933. He became the 44th Speaker of the House from 1931 to 1933 before becoming vice president in 1933. A prominent lawyer before embarking on his political career, he was an avid outdoorsman who spent considerable time hunting and fishing in his beloved state.

Although Garner served two terms under FDR as vice president from 1933 to 1941, he opposed many of Roosevelt's "New Deal" spending policies. The two men had a serious split in 1937 and were never able to reconcile their differences. When FDR ran for an unprecedented fourth term in 1940, Garner was not on the ticket.

A TEXAS DEER HUNT

◄ ROUGHING IT IN SOUTH TEXAS, LATE 1930s

With most of their gear unpacked from the trailer attached to the 1935 Chevy Master Deluxe four door, these hardy Texans are ready to pitch their tent and set up camp for an exciting week of chasing Lone Star bucks in the spectacular brush country of South Texas.

▲ COOKIE KNOWS HIS STUFF

How many groups of hunters have the foresight to bring along a camp cook with them? Apparently these Texans know the importance of eating well while roughing it in the wilds of the brush country. With a complete kitchen set up in the tree behind him, a grill to cook on and a good fire that will allow the big pot of stew to simmer, it's doubtful this seasoned cook will let anybody down. He surely plans to provide plenty of tasty vittles for the hungry crew of deer hunters in the days ahead.

SPOILS OF THE HUNT

After several days of watching the sun rise and witnessing breathtaking sunsets in God's country, the crew is more than happy to show off the spoils of another successful hunt. Every group of hunters has its "camp clown," a man who feels compelled to show off his jug of white lightning and bottle of spirits, and this group is no different. Note the small bodies on these deer, so typical of South Texas.

❮ HOMEWARD BOUND

Another great hunt has come to an end, but the memories of the week will last a lifetime. Having secured their deer to the front of the car, the men make sure their single Lone Star longbeard is prominently displayed on the hood as they pose for the camera one last time before heading back to civilization and the mayhem of the big city life.

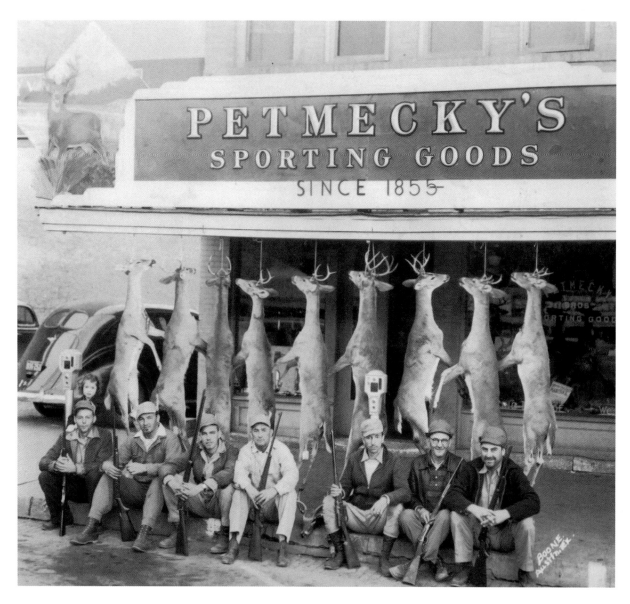

▲ A HEAP OF TEXAS FAJITAS

This 1937 photo, taken on the curb in front of Petmecky's Sporting Goods Store in downtown Austin, Texas, shows an impressive number of Lone Star bucks – 10 to be exact – and the lucky hunters who bagged them. From left to right, the hunter's first names are: Leslie, Buddy, Jake, Hal, Harold, Coke and Joe. Most of the rifles are classic Winchester lever-action rifles of various models, but Hal has a bolt-action sporter, possibly a Springfield Armory Model 1903, and Harold is wielding a venerable Remington Model 8. Note the sign in the store window that reads: "We rent guns." Imagine seeing that sign in a store these days!

Petmecky's was one of the oldest and most popular sporting goods stores in Austin during the first half of the 20th century. Family patriarch Joseph Carl Petmecky came to Texas as a boy in 1845. By the time the Civil War started in 1861, he was a respected gunsmith in Austin. By 1900, he was one of the best-known gunsmiths and gun dealers in all of Texas, selling his highly esteemed wares to Texas Rangers, hunters and cowboys alike.

For many years during the early 1900s, Joseph's son, Jacob Henry Petmecky, owned and operated this well-known Austin landmark. It was always a popular gathering place for hunters during deer season.

Dear Sam:

We'll have to go hunting again when I get back —

He's been doing a different kind of hunting overseas. But in between times, when he writes a letter to his loved ones, it's the *little* things he writes about.

The hunting trip, when he got the deer he's still so proud of . . . the grilled steak suppers in the backyard . . . the ship model he was working on before he left.

These are the little things that he looks forward to returning to. For it's the little things — the small familiar pleasures — that to him as to all of us, add up to home.

It happens that to many of us these important little things include the right to enjoy a refreshing glass of beer. Cool, sparkling, friendly, beer is a sign of satisfaction . . . a firm-set mouth relaxing into a friendly smile.

How good it is . . . as a beverage of moderation after a hard day's work . . . with good friends . . . with a home-cooked meal.

A glass of beer or ale—not of crucial importance, surely . . . yet it is little things like this that help mean home to all of us, that do so much to build morale—ours and his.

Men of the Marine Corps say letters keep up morale . . . Write that V-Mail letter today.

Morale is a lot of <u>little</u> things

◁ A GREAT DAY IN
THE BRUSH COUNTRY

Holding his scoped Winchester Model 70 bolt action, this beaming Texas hunter has bragging rights to a fine buck and a brace of hefty javelinas in the back of the truck. It's been a productive morning, and now it's time to round out the day by getting the deer and javelinas hung up in the barn, grabbing the double gun in the back of the truck and heading out for a little afternoon quail hunting. Just as it is today, South Texas has long been a true sportsman's paradise. Photo circa early 1950s.

▷ HOME FROM
THE HILL

Standing under a mesquite tree, Howard Knowles, a salesman at Crouch Hardware Company in Ft. Worth, Texas, poses with a young 8-pointer taken in South Texas. Wearing a pair of well-worn, calf-high Maine hunting boots with rubber bottoms (sold by L. L. Bean) and holding his dependable Savage Model 99 lever action, the pensive, pipe-smoking Mr. Knowles conveys the confidence that he has hunted in the brush country once or twice before. Compared to their northern cousins, Texas deer are typically much smaller in body size. It is doubtful this buck weighed more than 100 pounds field dressed. Photo circa 1950.

▲ **LONE STAR CACTUS HEAD WITH A SMOKEPOLE**

No, it's not Davy Crockett at the Alamo. The unusual buck was taken in South Texas by long-rifle hunter J.B. Eggleston on the second day of the season in November 1949. Wearing a coonskin cap and vintage buckskin clothing, 63-year-old Eggleston, a lover of primitive weapons, was using a homemade muzzleloader when he downed this 20-point nontypical whitetail. This wild looking velvet rack looks more like an inverted king crab or giant spider than a typical "cactus head" rack on a white-tailed deer, and it surely drew plenty of attention after it was brought down.

Cactus head bucks never shed their antlers or their velvet. The antlers sometimes continue to grow and bulb out at a slow rate. The condition is caused by an injury to one or both testicles, resulting in full or partial castration. The condition is often the result of a buck getting caught as he jumps over a barbed wire fence. Occasionally the injury comes from fierce fighting with other bucks. Cactus heads are often referred to as freaks of nature, but no noble whitetail buck – past or present – deserves such a demeaning title. Eggleston's trophy is a beauty!

THIS GIRL KNOWS HOW TO SHOOT
This poised young woman epitomizes Diana the huntress of Greek legend. The self-assured expression on her face tells us that she has declared ownership of at least one of the fine bucks hanging on the buck pole. She is in her element. Photo circa 1915.

> **The whitetail is a familiar figure throughout practically every state in the Union, nor is it necessary to undergo danger and hardship in bringing him to bag. Yet, when all is said (and I believe the much traveled sportsman will agree with me), there is no doubt about the fact the this noble member of our great deer family, by the very reason of his wide distribution, occupies a warm place in the hearts of the American people, and that skill and patience are essential if we would hunt him successfully in a legitimate fashion. To the man or woman therefore whose zest in following a game trail is quite as keen as those whom fortune has granted larger opportunities, he offers, and will continue to offer, splendid sport.**

Paul Brandreth
Trails of Enchantment, 1930
"Paul Brandreth" was a pen name of the gifted writer, Paula Brandreth, who because she was a female, felt the need to write under a man's name so that she could be published.

CHAPTER 13

ONE FOR THE LADIES

Through thick and thin, good times and bad, women have always been there for their men, ready to make any sacrifice and do anything necessary to help maintain a homestead and feed and protect the family. During the early days of settlement and steady westward movement, men did most of the necessary subsistence hunting and physical work while the womenfolk stayed home and held down the farm. Courageous women often single-handedly took on numerous vital and sometimes life-threatening tasks – nursing sick children, minding and protecting the garden from a variety of critters, and fighting ever-present natural elements that often appeared out of nowhere – flash floods, sweeping prairie and forest fires, life-threatening tornadoes, blizzards, treacherous windstorms, buffalo stampedes, swarms of grasshoppers and other perils of nature. Then, too, women had to deal with and even fight off hostile Indians.

Women who hunted deer and other game were not a common sight 100 years ago – but they were present nonetheless. In the late 1800s, these women were often referred to as "Dianas," in reference to the revered Roman goddess of the hunt, a considerable compliment indeed. Art pieces often depict Diana as a beautiful

young woman in a flowing gown carrying a bow and arrow and standing over a large stag she had slain.

By the early 1900s, as the once very necessary subsistence hunting slowly gave way to sport and meat hunting, women began to join their men on annual fall excursions into the deer woods, often camping and roughing it right alongside their menfolk. As hunting lodges slowly began to appear during the late 1800s in popular hunting destinations like northern Maine, the Adirondacks, and the North Woods of Michigan, Minnesota and Wisconsin, conditions were more conducive for women, and a growing number of ladies began to join their husbands for the annual fall trip to deer camp. Many of these ladies made a name for themselves with their ability to shoot straight and bring down the largest bucks in the area, frequently outdoing their husbands and the other men in camp.

Nonhunting women often got together and visited deer camp, bringing in fresh supplies and special desserts for the men, pies and cakes and other delicacies that normally would never be seen in such a wild and woolly setting. They would sometimes stay a day or two and prepare special meals, much to the enjoyment of the men. After all of the hunting was finished, women often spent long hours helping their men cut up and package the meat to prepare it for cooking, and curing in the smokehouse.

The 21st century has seen a huge increase in the number of women joining their husbands and boyfriends, fathers, brothers, uncles, cousins and children in the woods, and playing a much larger role in whitetail hunting across America.

Ironically, many of these women are very proficient bowhunters, something that would have turned quite a few heads of rifle-toting females back in the late 19th and early 20th centuries. But, the rich heritage of the fairer sex conquering the deer woods goes back well into the 1800s, and we can thank those courageous and rugged pioneer women for paving the way so long ago.

◄ A DANDY BUCK FOR A REFINED LADY

With her Winchester rifle planted firmly on the ground in front of her, this well-dressed lady proudly shows off an enormous 10-point buck taken in northern Maine. Since she does not appear to be dressed for the occasion, we must ask, is this her buck? She certainly seems to impart ownership. Remember, during the Gilded Age that lasted from about 1870 into the early 1900s, both men and women often were seen in remote hunting camps in their everyday city attire; suits for the men and fancy dresses for the ladies. This postcard was made in the early 1900s.

ALL THE COMFORTS OF HOME

With a tent in the background and a cooking fire in the foreground, these two sturdy and resolute pioneer women are right at home in a wilderness camp far off the beaten path. The weather is mild, indicating this scene may be somewhere in a more southern climate. The man is holding two chained dogs, a muzzled pit bull and an obedient hound that no doubt played a role in chasing down the fine twosome of venison on the hoof.

While the gentleman clutches a trusty double-barrel shotgun that has been responsible for collecting its fair share of meat, the lady on the left is very proud of her lever-action Marlin Model 1893. The lady in the middle appears to also be holding a shotgun.

BIG BULLET FOR A LITTLE LADY

It takes the right bullet and a plenty of confidence to bring down a thick-antlered trophy whitetail like this outstanding 10-pointer, and this young lady sure has both. No, this isn't Annie Oakley, but this proud female hunter would give "Little Miss Sure Shot" a run for her money because she obviously knows how to hit a large whitetail with ease, and she's not afraid to use a powerful, shoulder-punishing bullet. She is very proud of her smooth-shooting Savage Model 99, likely chambered in .303 Savage, .30-30 Winchester or .38-55 Winchester, all popular in the late 1800s and early 1900s.

A WELCOME VISIT

Although many hardy outdoors women marched to a different drummer by actually braving the elements and hunting right alongside their men, others supported the cause by visiting camp. Since the members of a remote club like this Deep South hunting camp might be away from home for a week or longer during the fast-paced season, the womenfolk often brought food and other supplies, and even stayed around to do a little much-appreciated cooking. Photo taken in Mississippi, circa early 1900s.

BEAUTY AND THE BUCK

With her self-loading Winchester Model 1907 and furry white mittens, this attractive young lady is the envy of camp. The deer is wearing a metal antler tag typical of those used in Wisconsin beginning in 1920. One thing is certain – the husband or boyfriend of this lovely deer hunting lass is one lucky fellow! Photo circa 1920.

A LADY AND HER BUCK

Seasoned whitetail hunter Georgia Holtzclaw poses proudly with the result of another successful hunt made near La Pine, Ore., located in the central part of the state. Mrs. Holtzclaw is holding a classic Winchester lever action with a half magazine, likely a Model 53 produced from 1924 to 1932. It was available in only one style, the Sporting Rifle with a 22-inch round barrel. Photo circa late 1920s to early 1930s.

A HUNTING WE WILL GO

This scene indicates a family homestead in the Midwest in the early 1900s, perhaps Iowa or Wisconsin? Everyone is well armed, and the buck pole is full. The two ladies on the right are holding .22 rifles, very efficient small-game getters in the early 20th century, while the stalwart lady on the left handles a shotgun. The three men are all armed with lever-action rifles. Judging by the belt knifes and ax, this group has been doing some serious whitetail hunting in late summer or early fall when it was time to put up as much meat as possible for the coming winter. Photo circa 1900-1910.

◄ **MICHIGAN'S DEAR HUNTING QUEEN**

◄ **MICHIGAN'S DEAR HUNTING QUEEN**

Posed in front of a hunting lodge displaying a couple cases of beer in the background, including the popular Stroh's Bohemian Beer brewed in her home state, Mildred Stemlund of Rapid River, Mich., shows off the buck that earned her the local title of "Dear Hunting Queen." Photo circa 1948.

> **AN EXTRAORDINARY OUTDOOR LADY AND NOTED HUNTING GUIDE**

Wearing a beautiful buckskin jacket and holding a sporterized Springfield Armory Krag-Jorgensen .30-40 rifle, 19-year-old Marie Sarkipato Ericson of Ely, Minn., poses with a large doe taken in northern Minnesota in December 1938. During the late 1930s, '40s and '50s, Marie was a skilled canoe guide who often led long trips into the Boundary Waters area. She also ran a family resort on a popular area lake. An avid outdoorswoman, the blonde beauty had recently married and was serving as a hunting guide in a remote camp when this photo was taken.

The Minnesota Tourist Bureau featured Marie in a number of stories promoting tourism in northern Minnesota and she became quite well-known in the area. She also had a feature story written about her in *Look* magazine in February 1938. One newspaper article titled "Minnesota's Beautiful Girl Guide Hits the trail in the North Woods," written in the spring of 1938, told about how Marie celebrated her 19th birthday by guiding several other ladies on a 100-mile canoe trip that began at Fall Lake near Winton, Minn. Marie eventually moved to Chugiak, Alaska, where she spent the latter years of her life. For many years during the 1980s and '90s, she returned to Minnesota annually to visit old friends.

⌃ ONE FOR THE LADIES

Althea Vigue of Waterville, Maine, shows off her 200-pound, heavy beamed 6-pointer taken during a special October hunt in 1939 before the regular statewide season opened on Nov. 1. Althea is proudly holding a Winchester Model 53 lever action. Manufactured between 1924 and 1932, this popular model was discontinued in 1932 due to lackluster sales caused primarily by the Great Depression and the fact that it could not compete with the enormous popularity of the Model 1894.

The Model 53 came in three calibers: .44-40, .32-20 and .25-20. The .25-20 was a widely used cartridge for whitetails during the early 1900s and may well have been what Althea was hunting with on that unforgettable day in the Maine woods. If so, she was in good company. Twenty-five years earlier in November of 1914, a young man named James Jordan was hunting near Danbury, Wis., with a Winchester Model 1892, the precursor to the Model 53, chambered in .25-20 caliber when he downed what was destined to become one of the greatest whitetails of all time. Many years later in 1966, the Jordan buck was declared a world record typical with an official Boone and Crockett score of 206⅛ points.

AN ASPIRING ANNIE OAKLEY

Arising early at her home on the family farm in Windsorville, Maine, on the morning of Nov. 24, 1938, 17-year-old Augusta High School senior Catherine Turner looked out the bedroom window and saw this beefy 8-point buck feeding in a field 150 yards away. Resting her father's tried-and-true Winchester Model 94 on the window sill, she dropped the deer in its tracks. Miss Turner's outstanding buck reportedly weighed 250 pounds and was said to be one of the largest taken in the vicinity of Augusta during the 1938 season.

Catherine's Winchester Model 94 was well used and obviously accurate. Throughout the first half of the 20th century, Winchester was the gun of choice in Maine and across New England. In fact, a decade before she downed her memorable buck, the one-millionth Model 1894 Winchester lever-action rifle was presented to President Calvin Coolidge in 1927.

HE'S ALL MINE BUSTER

This happy lady admires a young 8-pointer resting across the hood of the family Nash sedan bearing a 1949 Washington state license plate. The two rifles crossed in front of the car – a scoped Savage Model 99 and a sporterized bolt-action 1903 Springfield – suggest at least two hunters. Since she is wearing a wool hunting jacket, she most certainly could have been in on the hunt.

PRIZE DOE BY BOW

A smiling Leona Dresser (center), wearing a plaid Mackinaw, poses with her recurve bow and the wooden arrow that was responsible for bagging this prize doe. Her deerskin-jacket-wearing husband, Harry Dresser (left), and hunting companion Frank McLeod, assist in getting her deer out of the woods. The Dressers often hunted as nonresidents in Wisconsin and were quite skilled at bowhunting for deer in the great Dairy State. Photo dated 1956.

ROSIE THE RIVETER GOES DEER HUNTING

It is a fine autumn day in the Michigan woods in 1942 and this smiling young lady has done herself proud by bagging a healthy young 4-pointer. Across her lap rests a trusty Savage lever action, a great choice for any hunter. Is her husband and the men in her family off fighting in Europe or the Pacific? We don't know the answer to that, but one thing is certain — she can certainly hold her own in the Michigan deer woods.

READY TO LEAD THE CHARGE

The distinguished gentleman on the right is reminiscent of a Civil War colonel about to lead his faithful rebel raiders into battle. In fact, he might well be a veteran of that war. For certain, he is a veteran of many a deer chase through the wild Mississippi swamps. There is little question that he can handle himself in the saddle.

"At first there was nothing. There was the faint, cold, steady rain, the gray and constant light of the late November dawn, with the voices of the hounds converging somewhere in it and toward them. Then Sam Fathers, standing just behind the boy as he had been standing when the boy shot his first running rabbit with his first gun and almost with the first load it ever carried, touched his shoulder and he began to shake, not with any cold. Then the buck was there. He did not come into sight; he was just there, looking not like a ghost but as if all of light were condensed in him and he were the source of it, not only moving in it but disseminating it, already running, seen first as you always see the deer, in that split second after he has already seen you, already slanting away in that first soaring bound, the antlers even in that dim light looking like a small rocking chair balanced on his head."

William Faulkner
"The Old People," from *Big Woods*, 1955

CHAPTER 14

A MISSISSIPPI BIG-WOODS DEER CAMP

Whitetail hunters have their idiosyncrasies and famed writer William Faulkner (1897-1962) was no exception. Each November, he relished going to deer camp in the Mississippi Delta country several hours drive from his home in Oxford, Miss. There he would spend 10 glorious days forgetting the pressures of the outside world and just be one of the boys among the hard-living, hard-drinking and hard-hunting deer hunters who made up the members of his hunting club.

When word came in November 1950 that he had won the Nobel Prize in Literature, he wrote a hasty reply letter to the Swedish Academy saying he would not be able to attend the awards ceremony. Nothing was going to get in the way of going to deer camp. Several of Faulkner's best short stories, including "Race at Morning" and "The Old People," were based on his cherished experiences in deer camp during the 1930s, '40s and '50s. Like Archibald Rutledge of South Carolina, William Faulkner was able to capture the true essence of Deep South deer hunting in Mississippi through his timeless words.

The following collection of photos was taken in the early 1900s, a little before Faulkner's time.

The one-of-a kind photos depict a typical big-woods deer camp in the early 1900s, at a time when Faulkner was a still small boy learning how to shoot a rifle.

The Quest and the Quarry

Each man had his reasons for going to deer camp in November, reasons that were as varied and complex as life itself. Most enjoyed getting away from the complicated demands of normal life for a week or longer and living close to nature, reliving their boyhood days to some degree by shooting guns, riding horses and hunting deer. At deer camp they could be themselves. The camaraderie of deer camp was equally important, along with the challenges of hunting a crafty animal and spending time alone in the woods for a few hours to clear the mind and re-energize the soul.

In the end though, it came down to one thing: these men were deer hunters, and no man in camp would be satisfied unless he had a fine buck hanging on the pole at the end of the week. Making the difficult shot, being esteemed by one's companions and going home with confidence in one's abilities – these were the primary reasons for being there. Whitetails were their addiction and spending time in a big woods camp was their remedy, the real reason they came back year after year.

A Deep South Tent City Deer Camp

From the late 1880s into the early 1900s, hunting club members often erected "tent city" deer camps that could accommodate up to 20 hunters in remote areas for a week or longer. Hunters would come and go during the November season as their time permitted. Common amenities usually included a large cook tent where all of the meals were prepared. An equipment tent or an area covered by a large tarp was also a necessity in order to protect saddles and bridles, bales of hay for the horses and other items that needed to stay dry. Any number of sleeping tents would be set up to accommodate hunters.

A large campfire circle in the center of camp would serve as the community center. The men would sit around the fire at night, swap stories and usually partake in a few rounds of "blizzard medicine," or hard moonshine. The horses would be picketed on ropes a few yards away in the woods and a buck pole to hang the deer would be set up in one corner of camp. A designated area for the hounds would also be a few yards away in the woods.

Many of the original tent city camps were transformed into more permanent camps during the 1920s and '30s. Rustic camp clubhouse structures were erected that replaced the old tents. Nothing too elaborate was ever built because the delta country was subject to flooding nearly every year, and a primitive hunting lodge, if still standing at all, might end up with 2 or 3 feet of water in it.

Many of the club members were local farmers in the Mississippi Delta area. Some were local businessmen or men with other odd occupations – like William Faulkner the writer – who loved the camaraderie of deer camp. Many of these early camps grew into large multigenerational clubs where grandfathers, fathers and uncles passed the torch to sons and cousins.

Some still flourish today.

> **ON THE HUNT**
With his Browning Auto-5 shotgun and cow horn with which to call in the dogs, this seasoned huntsman is ready to get on with the chase.

⋀ POSING BY THE BUCK POLE

Most club members hunted off of horseback, following the hounds deep into the Mississippi swamps. Often the riders would shoot at a running deer right off the horse's back, provided the horse was trained for such an endeavor. Otherwise a hunter might find himself on the ground and his mount headed for the next county. The high vantage from a horse's back offered a good view of the surrounding woods, a decided advantage when deer came bounding by. It also kept a man from having to deal with pesky little ground critters like water moccasins and alligators.

Some hunters opted to dismount in the woods, tie their horses in an out-of-the-way thicket and take a ground stand, waiting for the dogs to push the deer by their position.

HAULIN' 'EM IN

BRINGIN' IN ANOTHER ONE
A faithful horse carries the day's prize for these weary but happy Southern buck hunters.

PACKIN' 'EM OUT

Instead of having to drag a buck out of the woods in the traditional way, Mississippi Delta hunters used horses and mules for the job. While some beasts of burden are terrified at the smell of blood, this sturdy mule apparently has been trained well, and isn't bothered in the least by the outstanding buck on its back.

TENT CITY

▲ A board of directors meeting in deer camp.

▲ A neat and well-organized camp indeed.

➤ **IT WOULDN'T BE CAMP WITHOUT A FIRE**
The campfire circle was the social center of camp, especially in the evenings.

Hunters could always count on rain and mud in deer camp, so this innovative crew constructed its own walkway with large planks.

⌃ Another view of tent city.

⌃ Preparing to head out to the woods for the afternoon hunt.

◁ WHAT'S
FOR SUPPER?

The cook tent was the most popular place in camp, unless there were dirty dishes that needed washing.

BIG-WOODS BOUNTY

△ Nice buck! Couldn't be happier!

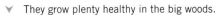
▽ They grow plenty healthy in the big woods.

▽ Definitely a keeper.

△ Two for two!

The youngest hunter always seems to get the largest buck.

A proud hunter with a dandy ol' swamp buck.

One of the camp patriarchs with a true patriarch of the woods.

There's always a time to reflect at the end of the hunt.

BIG-WOODS CHARACTERS

Deer camp is enough to wear a man out.

▲ Rigging the buck pole.

▲ Deer camp characters.

⋏ Admiring the prize.

⋏ A big-woods bear was fair game too.

ᐱ All the gang wants in on the photo of the biggest buck of the hunt.

ᐱ Ask anyone of the deer camp crew – there's no finer place on earth.

A MICHIGAN KEEPER

Carl W. Runyan of Buchanan, Mich., caught up with this wide-spreading monster on Nov. 18, 1942, while hunting in the wilds of Iron County in the Upper Peninsula. With an outside spread of nearly 30 inches and an inside spread of 28-4/6 inches, Carl's unique trophy won first place in a 1942 big deer contest sponsored by the *Detroit Free Press* for having the widest spread and the most points of any rack entered. With an official Boone and Crockett score of 230-5/8 nontypical inches, the buck still ranks as one of Michigan's great nontypicals of all time. Today the impressive trophy is owned by Bass Pro Shops and can be seen as part of its Legendary Whitetail collection in Springfield, Mo.

> **With the crisp days of early October, the buck is a picture of robust health, exuberant vitality, and lordly mien. His swollen neck adds to his pugnacious appearance, and he becomes a bit daring in his well-being, for now he steps forth from his usual obscurity and stalks in his domain with some measure of arrogance.**

George Mattis
Whitetail – Fundamentals and Fine Points for the Hunter, 1969

CHAPTER 15

LAND OF MANY GIANTS

Since prehistoric times, those animals possessing horns, tusks or antlers have always had a spellbinding influence on the humans who hunted them for food. Early man devised countless uses for horns and antlers, and great importance was placed upon those sacred pieces of bone that crowned the heads of various creatures. Today, things are no different. No portion of a whitetail's anatomy holds more esteem to the All-American deer hunter than an impressive set of "rocking chair" antlers.

While few hunters of yesteryear ever considered themselves to be trophy hunters, it was always a special occurrence when someone dragged a buck into camp sporting a huge set of "horns." Trophy racks were much more likely to be seen in the North where the body sizes of deer were historically larger than those of their cousins in the South. But, above-average antlers were apt to be, and were, found almost anywhere whitetails lived. Trophy deer came from every corner of the country where whitetails tantalized and frustrated hopeful hunters. They came from the Northern Great Lakes, from Maine to Montana and across southern Canada. They came from the Northeast and the farm belt. They came from Texas and the Southeast.

Just when a hunter expected it the least, a giant buck would step out and a new hunting hero would be born. Although the vast majority of men hunted for meat a century ago, a few driven souls in the early 20th century did find great pleasure in searching the land for massive antlered bucks.

To most hunters, the excitement generated by sighting a live deer in the woods is a remarkable thing. If that deer happened to possess a good set of "horns," strange things began to happen. Buck fever, commonly referred to as the "ague" 100 years ago, might cause a hunter to lose all sense of control – just as it often does today.

In the end, if a hunter is fortunate enough to wind up with an impressive set of trophy antlers to hang on the wall, those antlers will be but one of many rewards derived from his passion and painstaking efforts.

JAMES JORDAN'S GREAT "SANDSTONE" BUCK

On Nov. 20, 1914, 22-year-old Jim Jordan of Danbury, Wis., shot a massive buck while hunting near the Yellow River with an 1892 Winchester lever-action .25-20 WCF. The buck had an enormous rack and young Jordan decided to part with $5 and have it mounted by taxidermist George Van Castle in Webster, Wis. That would be the last time he would see his trophy rack for 50 years. Van Castle moved out of state, and the deer disappeared.

Through a series of incredible events, in 1958 the huge rack was bought at a rummage sale in Sandstone, Minn., just north of where the taxidermist Van Castle had once lived in Hinckley, Minn. Jordan and his trophy were eventually reunited – although someone else had bought the rack by that time – and the rack was scored for the Boone and Crockett Club record book. At an unbelievable 206⅛ typical points, it became a new world record. Since Jordan had no hard proof that he had killed the deer way back in 1914, Boone and Crockett was reluctant to credit him as the hunter. In 1978, when the club finally saw fit to recognize him as the hunter who had killed the giant deer, he had recently passed away.

Jordan never lived to receive the recognition he so deserved. Wisconsin's great Sandstone buck, taken by James Jordan, reigned as the world record typical until 1993, at which time Canadian hunter Milo Hanson shot an enormous buck in Saskatchewan that scored 213⅝ points.

A WISCONSIN MYSTERY BUCK

We think it's from Wisconsin – but we know it's a giant! This sensational buck is a main-frame 6-by-6 with a split G-3 on the right and a small sticker point on the left G-3. The century old trophy probably has a gross score in the middle to high 170s. The right brow tine easily measures 7 to 8 inches in length. Whoever shot this great buck knew it was special and had the forethought to get the deer mounted and properly photographed in a studio for future generations to admire. Thank goodness classic photographs like this survive to this day.

This vintage cabinet card photo was taken between 1910 and 1925 in the studios of the Schubert Brothers, who had locations in Kiel and Chilton, Wis., during the late 1800s and early 1900s. Fred and Paul Schubert were very well-known photographers and they made hundreds of stunning portraits from glass negatives.

THE SWIMMER

Whitetails have always been known to be strong swimmers, and big bucks often seek bodies of water to escape danger. They frequently swim across rivers and lakes, often traveling long distances across waterways. This photo came out of the Fred Goodwin collection, and was probably taken in the 1930s or '40s. Fred often traded photos with other "horn men" in other states. He received this photo from fellow antler collector Widmer Smith of Hayward, Wis.

The huge buck was captured on film at Clam Lake, just north of Loretta, Wis. Judging from the long tines on this massive 10-point velvet rack, this buck was definitely a record-book contender. Was the deer eventually taken by a hunter? Or, did he die of old age in the vast forests and swamps of the area like bucks of this caliber often do? We can only speculate as to what this great buck's ultimate fate might have been. It is probably safe to say that few men have ever captured a truly giant buck like this on film in the open water.

HIGHEST SCORING 7-BY-7 TYPICAL EVER

Knoxville, Iowa, service station owner Lloyd Goad and his brother-in-law had been hunting deer with shotguns ever since the Iowa season opened in the early 1950s. In 1961, Lloyd decided to try his hand at hunting with a bow. He purchased a recurve bow and practiced whenever he could in one of the stalls at his gas station. That first season, he missed two bucks, but the challenge of hunting with a bow had grabbed him and wouldn't let go. The following year, he hunted nearly all season long without once pulling back his bow string.

On Dec. 2, 1962, the last day of the season, he decided to try one last time. As he entered the woods he saw several other hunters. This was not a good omen. He stopped next to an elm tree not far from a fence line and waited. Moments later, a massive buck came trotting through the woods and jumped the fence only 18 paces from where Lloyd was standing. Just as Lloyd released his wooden arrow, the deer spun around and the broadhead hit the deer's foot. Fortunately it severed an artery and the huge buck quickly expired.

The 224-pound buck sported a perfect 7-by-7 typical rack that later tallied 197-6/8 Pope and Young Club points, good enough to make it the new archery typical world record at the time. Three years later in 1965, Illinois bowhunter Mel Johnson shattered Lloyd's record by shooting a massive main-frame 6-by-6 giant near Peoria scoring 204-4/8 inches. Today, the Lloyd Goad trophy still holds the distinction of being the highest scoring 7-by-7 typical whitetail ever taken by a bowhunter.

TOO WIDE TO GET THROUGH THE FRONT DOOR

The father of five sons, John Breen worked as a store clerk in Bemidji, Minn., in the early 1900s. Being an avid deer hunter all his life, John Breen's family often feasted on venison. In 1918 when John was 52, a friend and customer named Knute Wick invited him on a November deer hunt near the town of Funkley, located about 30 miles north of Bemidji and about 70 miles south of the Canadian border. At the time, two of John's sons were serving in France during World War I.

John grabbed his gear and trusty Winchester .30-30 and hopped aboard a northbound train to join his friend in Funkley. In those days, a man could flag down the train at any point along its route and ride as far as he wanted to go for two cents a mile. When John returned home from his excursion a few days later, he had with him a buck so large in antler growth that it created quite a sensation in Bemidji. In fact, the deer's rack was so huge that John splurged and got the trophy head mounted by a taxidermist.

John's son Ray, 12 at the time, remembered that the rack was so wide that John had trouble getting it through the front door of the house. It had an inside spread of 23-5/8 inches. Ray also remembered that although huge in body size, the deer was gaunt and thin and its meat was so tough that it wasn't fit to eat. It was obviously well past its prime. "Nonetheless, we ate on that buck for so long that I hoped dad would never shoot another one like it," Ray said years later.

John died in 1947 at age 81. A decade later, friends urged several of the Breen boys to have the trophy measured for the national Boone and Crockett Record Book. With a score of 202 inches, the trophy became a new world record typical whitetail in 1960. It held that position until 1966 when another vintage buck, a main-frame 5-by-5 killed by an unknown hunter 200 miles away near Danbury, Wis., came to light. That buck measured 206-1/8 typical points, thus grabbing the No. 1 spot. It was later determined that a hunter named James Jordan had killed the newly crowned world record. Had it not been for six small abnormal points on the Breen rack (three on each side), it would have easily outscored the Jordan rack.

Today, nearly a century after it was killed, John Breen's "over-the-hill" giant still ranks within the top 10 typical whitetails of all time. While the meat might have been too tough to eat, the extraordinary rack has a surreal quality that to this day inspires a sense of awe, causing many antler experts to regard it as the greatest typical whitetail ever.

John Breen with his trophy in the snow.

Breen sons at the Boone and Crockett Club Awards Banquet in 1960.

The old, moth-eaten head was so enormous that it barely fit through the front doorway.

THE GREATEST TYPICAL WHITETAIL EVER TAKEN IN THE SOUTHEAST

In November 1961, an avid young outdoorsman named Buck Ashe from Chamblee, Ga., was out training quail dogs in Monroe County, about 80 miles south of Atlanta. Buck was an avid bowhunter with many fine whitetails to his credit. It just so happened that deer season was open, and several of Buck's friends were also in Monroe County deer hunting. They approached Buck and asked him to go with them the next morning. "I don't have my bow gear with me," Buck answered. "That's okay," one of his friends told him. "We have an extra rifle."

Buck reluctantly went along with his friends the next morning, carrying a borrowed Marlin .30-30. He went down to a creek bottom where he had previously found some good buck sign. Shortly after daylight, a massive buck came sneaking through the woods, and Buck dropped him with a single shot. The deer was huge and everyone urged Buck to get it scored for the record book. But because he had shot the deer with a rifle instead of his bow, he refused. Not until almost 40 years later in 1999 was the giant rack scored thanks to the efforts of Buck's son, Mark. The world-class 16-point rack tallied up 191-4/8 typical points, good enough to make it a Georgia record – as well as the largest typical whitetail ever taken in the Southeast.

POST-WAR BONANZA

Joe Haske hailed from a large family in central Wisconsin where hunting was a deeply rooted tradition. He and his four brothers grew up providing small game for the dinner table. By the time the five boys were grown, deer numbers had made a fairly strong comeback in Wood County where each of the men farmed for a living. By the mid-1940s, the five hard-working Haske boys loved to take a few hours off during deer season and conduct several opening-day deer drives that always produced plenty of venison.

During the summer of 1945, America had much to celebrate. Not only was World War II finally at its end, but Joe's 17-year-old son Roger and Joe's youngest brother John had glimpsed a sizable buck running around on the farm several times. When opening day of the short five-day season arrived on Saturday, Nov. 24, the five brothers were up at 4:30 a.m., anxious to start their first deer drive on a neighbor's woodlot as soon as it was light enough to see.

As one of three standers, Joe was in the process of making a wide circle around that woodlot in order to reach his designated position, when he crested a small hill and ran headlong into a buck that appeared to have a small tree

growing out of its head. Using a Savage .30-30, he made an instinctive snap shot on the running deer, hitting it in the hindquarters and knocking it down. Furious at himself for making such a poor shot, Joe quickly finished the business with a second bullet.

Although the buck's rack was bigger than any set of antlers Joe had ever seen, he had no plans to get the deer mounted because he thought it would cost too much. However, his brothers convinced him to do otherwise, each chipping in a dollar to help foot the taxidermy bill.

The mounted deer head proudly hung in Joe's home until he passed away in 1979. Eight years later in 1987, his daughter Joy agreed to have the incredible main frame 7-by-6 rack scored for the record book. The initial entry score was 204-2/8 typical points, but after being remeasured by a judge's panel at the Boone and Crockett Club's 20th Big Game Awards in 1989, that score was adjusted to 197-5/8 because of several incorrect calculations. Today the Joe Haske buck is regarded as one of Wisconsin's most revered typical whitetails of all time.

THE BRADY BUCK
THE LONE STAR STATE'S GREATEST WHITETAIL OF ALL TIME

Author's note: Much of the story behind one of the largest free-ranging bucks ever recorded in Texas, also known as the Benson Buck, the McCulloch Buck or the 78-point Buck, remains an unsolved mystery to this day. But the recently discovered photo shown here does shed some new light and perhaps adds a new piece to the puzzle. Several stories in books published in recent years cite different versions of what might have happened, but these stories are all sketchy at best. Since the events occurred between 100 and 125 years ago, we may never know the true facts.

Legend tells us that during the early 1890s, a number of working cowboys in and around the small central Texas town of Brady, in McCulloch County, reported seeing a whitetail buck possessing such a large "rack of horns" on its head that the deer was soon the talk of the town. Everyone wanted to shoot this deer. In late 1892, a local cowboy claimed he had shot and lost the deer. Jeff Benson, foreman for the vast Ford Ranch, was said to have found the deer and recovered its antlers. The massive antlers reportedly contained 80 points – later reduced to 78 points, and still later officially scored with 49 measurable points.

Benson reportedly brought the huge rack into Brady one day and asked a friend named Jim Wall who owned a feed store to sell it for him. Wall was said to have taken the massive rack down to San Antonio and sold it for $100 to well-known antler and curio collector Albert Friedrich (1864-1928), a German immigrant and saloon owner. Friedrich had acquired a local saloon

The author bought this rare photo of the original Brady Buck rack in an online auction about eight years ago. It was made in the late 1800s or early 1900s. The taxidermy work is not bad for the time period. It is probably safe to say that this photo has not been put before the public in nearly 100 years, if ever. Written on the back of the photo is the following:

"From collection at Buckhorn Saloon, Gonzales, Tex. Alex Schleyer, Prop.
Collection started in 1850. Valued $75,000.00
These Horns, The World's Record, 80 points
To Mr. C.C. Burns From Rolla B. Kinard, June 4, 1910."

As one of America's first serious antler collectors in the late 1800s, Albert Friedrich was passionate about his always expanding collection. He particularly sought unusual racks – cactus head bucks and freak racks with visible deformities. Even though the caption on the postcard reads, "A Pretty Group of the White and Blacktail Deer. To be seen at Albert's Buckhorn Saloon, San Antonio, Texas," most of the deer pictured are whitetails and mule deer.

about 10 years earlier in 1881 known as Albert's Buckhorn Saloon.

In order to draw more business, he decorated his saloon with hundreds of sets of deer antlers and horns from other animals that he avidly collected. Friedrich became the first large-scale antler collector, or "horn man," as he was called in those bygone days, in America. He once stated that he possessed "the largest and grandest collection of horns existing, native as well as foreign." At the time, that was probably an accurate statement. By 1900, he had amassed an enormous collection of antlers and curios from across the Southwest – including unusual furniture made from the horns of Texas longhorn steers and mosaics made from hundreds of rattlesnake rattles.

Word soon got out that a man could bring in a set of "deer horns" to Albert's Buckhorn Saloon and "swap" it for a drink. Cowboys, hunters and trappers began to pick up unusual antlers out on the prairie and bring them in on a regular basis. In the spring of 1898, while training in San Antonio before being shipped

down to Cuba to fight in the Spanish-American War, Theodore Roosevelt and his Rough Riders were said to have frequented the saloon on a regular basis.

Friedrich operated a thriving business until about 1920, when recently passed national prohibition laws made it illegal to sell alcohol. The ever-resourceful Friedrich relocated his business to Houston Street in 1922 and opened it up as Albert's Curio Store, where he sold all types of Texas memorabilia and unusual items. It was later known as the Buckhorn Curio Store and Cafe. Friedrich frequently used photos of the 78-point Brady buck to promote his business. That same year, he acquired a large antler collection owned by a man named Bill Keilman who had operated a similar saloon in San Antonio known as the Horn Palace. Included in the Keilman collection was a massive, 72-point nontypical deer head very similar to the one Albert already owned.

Bill Keilman died in 1926 and Albert Friedrich passed away two years later. If either man had known the precise history behind the

After Albert Friedrich obtained the shed antlers from the Brady Buck in the early 1890s, he had the "horns" mounted for display and attached to a star-shaped plaque with the letters "T-E-X-A-S" and "78 Points." By the turn of the century, Friedrich was marketing the gargantuan rack as a world record whitetail. The caption on the postcard reads: "The World's Champion. A Texas Deer Horn with 78 points. Albert's Buckhorn Saloon, San Antonio, Texas."

Photographed in 1986 by the author at the Buckhorn Hall of Horns at the Lone Star Brewery, this photo shows another angle of the 78-point shed antlers purchased by Albert Friedrich in 1895. Another 10 years would pass before this mount was found to contain the sheds – instead of the original rack.

78-point Brady buck and the more recently acquired 72-point set of antlers, that knowledge died with them. In 1956, Friedrich's children sold his vast collection of antlers and curios, including two of the largest sets of antlers ever seen in Texas, to the Lone Star Brewery in San Antonio. The collection was housed at the brewery and displayed as the popular "Buckhorn Hall of Horns." There it remained as a tourist attraction until 1998, when Albert Friedrich's grandchildren re-purchased the collection and displayed it in downtown San Antonio on Houston Street as the Buckhorn Saloon and Museum.

Shortly after acquiring Albert Friedrich's vast antler collection in 1956, officials at the Lone Star Brewery decided to have the two largest deer heads officially measured for the Boone and Crockett Record Book. Incredibly, Fried-

rich's first acquisition, the 78-point buck reportedly killed by a cowboy near Brady, Texas, in the early 1890s, tallied up a net score of 286 points – with a total of 49 measurable points, not 78. The 72-point buck tallied up 284⅜ net points – with a total of 47 measurable points, not 72. Both racks bested the existing nontypical world record at the time, a 245⅞ inch whitetail taken by Jim Brewster in British Columbia in 1905.

After having both deer entered in the Boone and Crockett Record Book, with the 286-inch Brady buck now reigning as the new world record nontypical, it became obvious to a growing number of people that the racks had to be related – one was an original while the other almost certainly had to be a set of sheds from that original. For reasons that defy explanation, instead of checking the skull plates of both racks

This postcard was widely distributed as a souvenir by the Lone Star Brewery during the 1960s, '70s and '80s. At the time, no one knew this mounted deer head actually contained the sheds of the Brady Buck instead of the original rack. After being officially scored in 1956 at 286 nontypical Boone and Crockett points, Albert Friedrich's legendary 78-point rack was actually credited with possessing 49 points over 1-inch long. This rack mistakenly remained the world's record nontypical from 1956 to 1996, at which time the trophy mount was X-rayed and found to contain shed antlers instead of an original skull plate. The caption on the back of the postcard reads: "78 Point Deer. This world's record whitetail deer was found in McCullough, County, Texas in 1892. The prize is displayed at the Buckhorn Hall of Horns, Lone Star Brewing Co., in San Antonio, Texas."

to find out for certain, the Boone and Crockett Club opted to drop the 284⅜-inch trophy from its listings.

Forty years later in 1996, thanks in part to the relentless work of official B&C measurer and Texas antler historian John Stein, both racks were X-rayed. You can imagine the shock wave that occurred when people realized that the 78-point Brady buck was found to be a set of sheds, while the 72-point trophy that Albert Friedrich had acquired from Bill Keilman was indeed the real McCoy.

This startling discovery spawned a Pandora's box of questions. Did Albert Friedrich know that the set of antlers he supposedly purchased from Jim Wall for $100 back in 1892 were in fact a set of sheds? He must have. But in fairness to Friedrich, he never made any claims about the deer either way. In those days, no one really cared, as no record books were then in existence. Friedrich simply called the trophy rack the "78-Point Buck" and from time to time people referred to it as a world record whitetail. But the discovery did seem to blow a hole in the legend about a cowboy shooting the deer and Jeff Benson finding the dead deer and recovering the antlers from the carcass.

The next obvious question that arises is where did Bill Keilman acquire the original set of antlers that he sold to Albert Friedrich in 1922? Part of that answer may be found in the turn-of-the century photo on page 210, bought in an online auction about eight years ago. An inscription on the back of the photo states that the rack had come from a "collection at the Buckhorn Saloon in Gonzales, Texas." The saloon's proprietor was Alexander Schleyer (1860-1949), a well-known taxidermist in the San Antonio area who collected antlers and was known to have provided and mounted many of the trophies for Albert Friedrich and the Lone Star Brewery. The back of the photo further states: "These horns – The World's Record, 80 points." The photo is dated June 4, 1910.

Based on the photo, it seems likely that Bill Keilman must have acquired the original rack of the Brady Buck from Alex Schleyer before he sold his collection to Albert Friedrich in 1922. We'll never know what transpired for certain. But we do know that somewhere around 1892, someone shot a truly amazing whitetail in Texas, the largest buck to ever walk the Texas plains. At some point along the way, either before or after that event, someone also found that deer's unbelievable shed antlers from the year before. Amazingly, both sets of antlers came together in 1922 and have remained together and on public display ever since.

Although there are still many unanswered questions about this great deer, one thing is certain – it's the largest free-ranging whitetail ever to come out of the Lone Star State!

THE SILVER RIDGE BUCK

Master whitetail hunter and guide Fred Goodwin poses with his massive "Silver Ridge" buck taken in Aroostook County, Maine, in December 1949. Fred hunted the big deer for three seasons after his brother Edwin missed a shot at the giant in 1946. The final hunt was bittersweet; Edwin, his brother and best friend in life, had died recently from cancer. This might have been the reason Fred decided to sell the antlers to one of his paying hunters. Although Fred was extremely fond of Winchester lever-action rifles, he killed the Silver Ridge buck with a classic Savage Model 99 in .300 Savage. Always ahead of his time, his rifle was equipped with a scope. Photo courtesy of Phil Osborne.

> In choosing a stand, take into consideration a place where you can rest your gun for a long shot. Should a deer pass through your line of vision without seeing you, do not hurry a shot if he's heading into a better spot. Bring your gun up slowly and be ready when he moves into what looks like the best possible location. If he's moving or loping along, make a slight clucking sound with your mouth. Almost without exception the deer will stop and throw its head up to locate the sound. Level your sights on the vital area and squeeze off the shot.

Fred Goodwin
The Art of Deer and Bear Hunting, 1953

CHAPTER 16

LAST OF THE HORN MEN

There's no doubt that Fred Goodwin (1909-2011) of Silver Ridge, Maine, was a chip off the old block. His father had an uncanny knack for buying low and selling high and always making a profit. Born in 1909, the 100th anniversary of Abraham Lincoln's birthday, Fred would live to be 102. He was like his father in many ways except for one. From his earliest boyhood recollections, he had a fascination for, and a burning passion to collect, deer antlers. Much to his father's chagrin, he began to collect and display old discarded antlers from neighbors who had shot deer for food.

His father, being a hard and practical man, insisted, "You can't eat deer antlers!" Once, at about the age of 13, after Fred had brought home yet another set of antlers to add to his growing collection, his father stormed upstairs to Fred's bedroom and threw all of his prized antlers out the window. Fortunately for Fred, a foot of snow covered the ground. After his father had retired for the evening, Fred sneaked outside and retrieved his cherished "deer horns."

A Horn Man in the Making

Thus began the saga of a larger-than-life individual who would become the greatest antler collector of the 20th century. Over the next 50 years, Fred traveled across New England and parts of Quebec to collect over 1,200 sets of trophy deer antlers, including many of the largest Maine whitetails ever killed by hunters. Knowing how important the history behind these deer was, Fred made sure he also collected the stories and tucked them away in his memory bank for the future. Many of the stories would have been lost for all time had he not had the foresight to remember the details.

Knowing that he was getting up in years, and also having a desire to see some of the racks in his collection recognized for what they were, Fred sold his entire antler collection in 1982 to collector Dick Idol of Montana. Dick rented a large truck to haul the unprecedented collection back to Montana. Of those 1,200 trophy racks, over 100 qualified for the Boone and Crockett Record Book.

Fred, who was always a very astute businessman and seldom got the worst end of any deal, actually sold the collection for a loss. At the time, there was little to no national market for such a large number of trophy deer racks, so he sold the entire collection that had taken him over half a century to amass for $25,000, or what amounted to about $20 per rack. Within a few short years, several of the racks in that collection sold for over $10,000 each. Today the entire collection would be priceless.

One of the many stories regarding record-book antlers that Fred salvaged occurred in 1934 when he was 25. At the end of hunting season, Fred customarily sent out letters to taxidermists, gun collectors and hunting guides across New England and parts of Quebec advertising the fact that he was interested in buying unusual or large antlers. People always needed money after the season was over so this was a good time to acquire antlers.

By chance, a very wealthy lady from Bangor named Mrs. Maney saw one of his letters and wrote him back that she had an old set of antlers he might be interested in purchasing. The deer had been killed just after the Civil War near the Reed Deadwater not far from Silver Ridge by a distant relative of hers, a Catholic priest named Father Maney from Danforth, Maine. This greatly sparked Fred's interest since he lived in Silver Ridge.

Months later, Fred accompanied his father and another man on a business trip to Bangor. At his earliest opportunity, he went to see Mrs. Maney. When she showed him the antlers, his eyes almost popped out of his head. They were huge. She was asking $5 for the rack but Fred had only $3 and some change in his pocket. Fred borrowed $2 from his father – who thought he was buying a gun. If he had known Fred was buying a set of antlers, he probably would have disowned his son on the spot. Fred went back and bought the rack for $5. He tried to hide it in the back of the truck on their trip home, but his father saw the rack and predictably went into a rage.

Years later, after Fred sold his entire antler collection, the Father Maney buck was officially scored at around 175 typical points. It reportedly sold to another antler collector for $8,500.

The Winchester Man for the Ages

Antlers were not the only items Fred collected. Early in his career he became a trader in guns, just like his father had been. Since Winchester lever-action rifles were the guns of choice for many hunters in Maine, Fred began trading for these rifles on a regular basis using the same successful strategies his father had always used.

During the Great Depression, most farmers in northern Maine customarily tried to lay up a supply of venison or moose meat for the winter. They would frequently buy a used Winchester lever-action rifle for $8 to $12. Then, after hunting season was over when the rifle was no longer needed, they would often go to Fred

THE ART OF DEER AND BEAR HUNTING

In 1953, Fred Goodwin and S. Stanley Hawbaker, a friend who sold lures and trapping supplies in Pennsylvania and often hunted with Fred in Maine, published this informative booklet. Much of Fred's savvy hunting wisdom is spelled out in the booklet.

Fred purchased the Father Maney buck for $5 in 1934 when he was 25 years old. It was one of the first of over 100 B&C bucks he would collect over the next 50 years. Although the old photo doesn't do it justice, the huge rack had a 30-inch spread and main beams measuring 30 inches in length. Photo courtesy of Phil Osborne.

and either "hock" the rifle or sell it outright for $4 to $6. The next year, just before the season opened again, Fred would sell those rifles back to the same hunters or other prospective hunters for $8 to $12, thus making a tidy profit.

As this cycle repeated itself year after year, Fred began keeping certain guns that were special or rare models. From about 1935 to 1970, Fred amassed a collection of Winchester lever-action rifles of every size and description – along with a respectable number of popular Winchester Model 70 bolt-action rifles – some 1,300 guns in all. There were saddle-ring carbines, long rifles, half-magazine models, guns with octagon barrels – virtually every model of rifle Winchester had ever produced. During the mid-1970s, 10 years before he sold his antler collection, fearing old age was settling in – little did he know he would live to be 102 – Fred sold the entire collection for several hundred thousand dollars.

Due to his passion for Winchester lever guns and his intimate work with them, Fred became one of the world's great authorities on these iconic rifles. Never missing an opportunity to make a dollar, he also began to collect spare parts from old rifles that were broken down

themselves almost without equal in accuracy and therefore carry a small calibre rifle in the belief that their extreme accuracy will enable them to place the small pellet in the brain of the game hunted, anywhere and anytime. The theory is that their small calibre rifle puts over the idea that they are accurate marksmen, veteran woodsmen and careful stalkers. For each person who can live up to this description, there are 100 who can't. Some of the best paper shooters do not stack up very well on fleeting glimpses of deer in heavy cover because most deer don't guarantee to stay in one place to give as much time as the 100-yard bull.

We have seen many deer taken as the result of poorly placed bullets from big calibre rifles. Small pellets from small calibre in the same spots would have often meant a cripple to crawl off and die. A deer that is left to die in the woods is of no value except for varmints or buzzard bait.

Go after trophy bucks when the rutting season is in.

This trophy buck was brought down at midday early in the rutting season.

A page from Fred's booklet shows an impressive Maine buck taken during the rut with his ever-dependable Savage Model 99.

Fact Sheet

FRED GOODWIN, LAST OF THE HORN MEN, (1909-2011)

- Larger-than-life whitetail hunter, trapper and guide from Silver Ridge, Maine. Lived to be 102 after an extraordinary life.
- The greatest white-tailed deer antler collector of all time. Sold his collection of 1,200 trophy antler sets to Dick Idol in 1982; over 100 B&C heads. He not only collected antlers, but also collected and preserved the stories of many of the trophy deer.
- One of the foremost collectors of Winchester rifles of the 20th century, and one of the world's great authorities on Winchester lever guns. Sold his collection of around 1,300 Winchester lever actions and Model 70s in 1972 for around $250,000. Made part of his living for many years selling Winchester parts.
- Gifted photographer, especially black and white landscape portraits. Many still survive today.

- Gifted artist, especially flat art, and a former tattoo artist with the circus in his younger days.
- Whitetail guide in Maine for over 40 years – 1936 to late 1970s. In 1936, he received $100 per week for five hunters.
- Skilled fur trapper and bounty hunter in Maine for more than 40 years. Caught record numbers of bobcats.
- Worked on the Alaska Highway during World War II with the Civilian Conservation Corps after a motorcycle accident left him unable to serve in the military. Made dozens of incredible photos of the highway being built that have never been published.
- Exceptional trophy whitetail hunter for 70 years. Shot numerous large whitetail bucks. Shot one of Maine's greatest bucks of all time in 1949 – the "Silver Ridge" buck.

and unsellable – springs, screws, levers, wooden stocks, buttplates and other pieces. Mostly by word of mouth, he started a very lucrative mail order business selling individual parts. In the late 1990s he was still filling orders that came in from all over the world.

The Great Silver Ridge Buck

Fred was a lifelong trophy hunter with many big bucks to his credit. He hunted moose and bear to some degree, but whitetails were always his passion. He killed his biggest buck ever, a massive whitetail known as the "Silver Ridge buck," in 1949.

In 1936, Fred and his brother Edwin, who was his best friend in life, started guiding "sports" from Pennsylvania and New Jersey during deer season. For many years the two brothers also trapped bobcat, beaver and other furbearing critters found in the region. Sadly, Edwin died

of cancer in the late 1940s, a tough time for Fred that he never got over.

During the 1946 deer season, Edwin missed a shot at a giant, wide-spreading buck. Fred hunted the buck for the next two years without success. Finally in 1949, after Edwin had passed away, Fred caught up with the old buck and put him down with one shot from his Model 99 Savage .300. Although its body was old and gaunt, the buck's rack was massive. A main-frame 6-by-6, Fred's Silver Ridge buck sported

FRED. GOODWIN

GUIDE & OUTFITTER   40 YEARS EXPERIENCE

DEER & BEAR HUNTERS CARED FOR IN NORTHERN MAINE WILDERNESS
CAMPS, CANOES, MOTORS & HORSES · EVERYTHING FURNISHED
RATES ON REQUEST

MONARDA,   MAINE.

One of Fred's business cards, circa late 1960s.

Fred posed with his beloved Silver Ridge Buck in the early 2000s when he was about 95 years old.

The author poses with Fred and Ida Goodwin and Fred's massive Silver Ridge buck in 2004 when Fred was 95. Fred regained possession of his beloved trophy 10 years earlier in 1994 after the Pennsylvania hunter he sold it to, Maylan Audiburt, passed away. Fred shot many trophy whitetails over the years, but this 1949 deer was his largest ever.

20 points and an inside spread of over 24 inches.

One of Fred's Pennsylvania hunters, Maylan Audiburt, happened to be in camp at the time. He talked Fred into selling him the rack for $100 under the condition that if he died before Fred, the rack would be returned to its original owner. In order to take it home with him on the train, Maylan had to split the skull plate into two pieces for easy transport.

Fred reluctantly parted with the rack. The recent loss of his brother Edwin was devastating, and this might have been part of the reason he decided to sell the rack since his beloved brother had also hunted the deer. As things turned out, Maylan died in 1994 and Fred was able to regain possession of the largest buck he had ever killed. By this time, there was much more interest in having big antlers scored for the record book. Since the skull plate had been split, however, the antlers were ineligible for entry into the record book. Nonetheless, Fred had the massive rack scored for his own purposes. The legendary Silver Ridge buck netted 239-4/8 nontypical points.

Fred was also a gifted photographer who took literally thousands of beautifully composed black and white photos during his lifetime. Many hundreds of those photos were classic hunting and trapping scenes in Maine. At the outbreak of World War II, Fred was turned away from joining the service because a serious motorcycle accident years earlier had left him with a badly broken leg. The leg never healed properly and was always shorter than the other. Undaunted, Fred joined the Civilian Conservation Corps just before it was disbanded by the government due to the war effort. He ended up spending many months working on the famed Alaska Highway, where he took hundreds of Ansel Adams-style photos of that historic roadway. During his spare time, he trapped wolves and hunted a variety of big game.

Fred went on to that great deer hunting paradise in the sky on Nov. 26, 2011. He would have been 103 years old in just 38 days.

HOPE FOR THE FUTURE

On Nov. 18, 1951, Ernie, who looks to be about 12 years old, shot his first deer, a fine young doe. Ernie was using a single-shot Savage 20 gauge. Today, if Ernie is still alive, he would now be in his late 70s. Let's hope he is still chasing whitetails, and that he has enjoyed a long lifetime of celebrating many opening days with his family and friends. Let's hope that the lessons learned on his first deer hunt stayed with him and were passed on to others over the years, so that the rich tradition of whitetail hunting across this great land will continue to flourish. And let's hope that many, many others continue to do the same.

"The whitetail's greatest future sport value is not just as big game, but as the common man's big game. It is available. It is a hometown, family budget, weekend sort of big game. It is the one great autumn adventure for millions of ordinary men hungry for personal, extraordinary adventure. Each year more of us yearn to the big woods and a contest that is ancient beyond our dimmest reckoning.

"The whitetail is here in quantity and is likely to remain so, just as long as hunters prize deer and autumn, and subscribe to the knowledge of their trained game managers and foresters."

John Madson
The White-Tailed Deer, published in 1961 by the Conservation Department of Olin Mathieson Chemical Company, East Alton, Ill.

CHAPTER 17

FROM SEA TO SHINING SEA
THE FUTURE OF DEER HUNTING IN AMERICA

Whitetails are the most emotion-stirring creatures on earth. For millions of Americans, whitetail hunting is truly the "last great adventure." But what will it be like in 50 years? 100 years? Perhaps we can answer that question in part by looking back at our roots. The dawn of deer hunting in America has come and gone, but maybe, in some small way, we can gain insight into the future by studying the past. We are fortunate, indeed, to be able to enjoy a glimpse back at the deer camps of yesteryear because of the thousands of photos like the ones in this book.

Our long and intermingled partnership with America's greatest game animal is unprecedented. There is no other story like it in the world. As with every aspect of American history, our deer hunting past is colorful and rich, but it has its blemishes. This alone should be reason enough to make every American hunter want to give something back, and do everything possible to protect this amazing resource for the future. It'll take work and dedication by people who understand good management and the hunting mystique. There will certainly be bumps in the road, but with a little American ingenuity and determination, two attributes that are part of the fiber of who we are as a people, the balance of the 21st century should play out to be just as colorful and exciting as the past 200 years.

Most nonhunting Americans have no idea how important whitetails have been in the shaping of our country. You simply have to be a hunter to fully realize and appreciate the impact of what these animals have done for our nation. Hunters must continue to stand at the forefront as they have always done and lead the charge into the future.

In the words of Jack Crockford, former director of the Game and Fish Commission of the Georgia Department of Natural Resources, and the man who developed the world-famous "Cap-Chur Gun" for deer in the 1950s:

"We should all remember how fragile a deer population is and how quickly it can be eradicated, thoroughly and completely."

May the future of deer hunting always be sunny and bright!

▲ AMERICA'S GREATEST GAME ANIMAL

What does the future of deer hunting in America hold? Will it be as rich as the past? Will the hunters of tomorrow still have the opportunity to go to deer camp and experience buck fever when a majestic animal like this steps out of the woods? If the good Lord's willing and the creeks don't rise, 100 years from now deer hunters of the future will still be experiencing the thrill of the chase and the raw emotion of confronting a whitetail buck. For this is the true essence of deer hunting.

NEW BEGINNINGS

Three hopeful bowhunters head out of camp to their afternoon stands as if they are walking off into the sunset. In a way, they were. While an old chapter of deer hunting in America had come to a close, a brand-new one was just beginning. These three hunters were taking part in the first ever archery-only hunt held in North Georgia's Rock Creek Refuge, now known as the Blue Ridge Wildlife Management Area, in October 1940.

This historic hunt received considerable national attention and news coverage because deer had been almost totally wiped out in the North Georgia Mountains by the late 1800s. Restocking efforts on national forest land started by renowned Forest Ranger Arthur Woody in 1927 resulted in a thriving deer herd by 1940, making this – the first deer hunt in modern times – possible.

This same story was played out over and over again in many parts of America. As a result, we are now reliving the good old days once more. Let's hope that we never see a time when whitetails are on the brink again.